Out of Control

Men, Women and Aggression

Anne Campbell

Pandora
An Imprint of HarperCollins*Publishers*
77–85 Fulham Palace Road,
Hammersmith, London W6 8JB

First published as *Men, Women and Aggression* by BasicBooks,
10 East 53rd Street, New York, NY 10022–5299, 1993
Pandora edition 1993
3 5 7 9 10 8 6 4 2

Material from *The Independent*,
April 23, May 16, and August, 1991,
reprinted with permission

A catalogue record for this book
is available from the British Library

ISBN 0 04 440885 4

Printed in Great Britain by
HarperCollinsManufacturing Glasgow

To Jamie

BY THE SAME AUTHOR

Girl Delinquents (1981)

Aggression and Violence (1982; co-edited with Peter Marsh)

The Girls in the Gang (1984; 2nd ed. 1990)

Violent Transactions: The Limits of Personality (1986; co-edited with John Gibbs)

The Opposite Sex (1989; edited)

CONTENTS

PREFACE

THE route that brought me to this book was long and circuitous. When I left university in England in 1972, I walked into my first job as a residential social worker to work with delinquent girls. The girls, I was informed, lived in one of two groups, the "blues" or the "greens." The blues were boisterous and aggressive; they were "acting out," in the vernacular of the profession. The greens were more withdrawn and more complex, given to self-injury and other less overt forms of "attention seeking." I chose the blues, feeling a more immediate sympathy with their anger and their confrontational approach to relationships.

As a conscientious psychology graduate, I went to the university library to find out more about female delinquency. But there was virtually nothing on the shelves. I struggled through a year of mostly exhausting and sometimes exhilarating work until I realized that without some coherent conceptual framework with which to approach these girls' problems, I would not get far.

I returned to the academic life to do a doctorate on female delinquency. The more I read, the more convinced I became that delinquency and aggression as expressed by women were simply incomprehensible to the male mind. Such women were seen as maladjusted because, it was assumed, they were acting like men. Aggression belongs to men, and women who venture into their arena are quickly dealt with by a two-pronged attack: question their deviation from femininity and thereby question their sanity.

With my doctorate behind me, I spent the next decade talking to the most aggressive young women I could find, mostly in remand centers awaiting court appearances or in juvenile or adult prisons. Mindful of the need for a control group, I also talked to nonviolent girls from similar backgrounds. I moved to the United States in 1979 to study girl gang members, and the dialogues in chapter 8 are taken from recordings I made of their conversations.

But in using control groups as an implicit base against which to search out the factors that give rise to aggression in young women, I was guilty of accepting the prevailing wisdom that normal women are not aggressive. Now it is certainly true that most women are not criminally violent, but very few women do not feel or act on anger, sometimes physically. In time I grew less interested in unusually violent women and more in the typical woman and her everyday experiences of anger and aggression. I read with increasing impatience the hundreds of experimental studies that had wrenched subjects away from the real world and into the laboratory. Although I knew that such studies were necessary, I needed to hear about people's experiences in their own words. So I armed myself with a tape recorder and began to listen to what people had to say about their own aggression. What I heard led me inexorably to ask, Why is aggression so different in men and women?

This book is my answer. Other theories explain the differences in terms of biological and hormonal effects, the way parents react to aggressive behavior in boys and girls, or the social requirements of gender roles. I believe that men and women differ in their aggressive behavior because of differences in how they come to understand the meaning of aggression. Women see aggression as a temporary loss of control caused by overwhelming pressure and resulting in guilt. Men see aggression as a means of exerting control over other people when they feel the need to reclaim power and self-esteem.

In chapter 1, I describe how culture transmits representations of everyday theories of aggression that differ for the two sexes. Individuals do not have to invent a theory about their aggression; it is all around them—in their daily conversations, in books, and on television. By adulthood, men and women inhabit distinct but parallel universes of aggression, and I trace the shaping of these understandings through childhood in chapter 2. In chapters 3 and 4 I eavesdrop on men and women talking to close friends about their experiences of anger and aggression. Whether it is righteous indignation about a repairman who shows up late or the final fury of a dying love affair, men and women may live in the same world but they understand the meaning and dynamics of aggression quite differently. As we will see in chapter 5, these different beliefs make aggression actually look different in men and women.

Gendered differences in social representations of aggression also emerge in the realm of serious injury and violence. In chapters 6 and 7, I examine two areas of violence: robbery, an overwhelmingly male activity, and domestic violence, which men and women engage in with equal frequency. I then tackle the paradox of young women in street gangs, examining how social forces can lead women to trade in their expressive view of aggression for an instrumental one. In the concluding chapter I focus on power, gender, and violence, showing how the patriarchal nature of our society legitimates men's theories of aggression while discounting women's as evil or irrational. The idea that women and men see and express aggression in different ways may be simple, but it has wide-ranging implications.

ACKNOWLEDGMENTS

WINSTON CHURCHILL once said that a book starts as a toy, becomes a lover, and ultimately turns into a tyrant. He was right. And it's not only the author who suffers under its despotic rule. That is why my first thanks go to my family for living with my obsession and my nightly absences during the last two years. It was a rough time in many ways. We changed continents and jobs and successively inhabited four homes. Through all this I insisted on dragging my file cabinet of references everywhere I went. My son was in diapers when I began this book and was a highly verbal four-year-old by the time I finished it. Each night he would fall asleep to the monotonous tapping of my word processor in the study.

Thanks go also to the individuals who contributed to the ideas in this book: to all my friends from Capulet's in Brooklyn, who gave me so much rich material on the meaning of aggression in their lives and who unwittingly sowed the seeds of this book's argument; to the gang girls with whom I spent two exhilarating years and who thought their contribution was finished when *The Girls in the Gang* was published in 1984; and to Steven Muncer, who generously shared with me his ideas on female desistance from robbery, which form the basis of many of the ideas in chapter 6. Jake Gibbs and Steven Muncer kindly organized and taped the men's group discussions quoted from in chapter 4.

I would also like to thank those who provided feedback. This includes students at Rutgers University in New Jersey and the University of Teesside, where courses in violence and research methods frequently turned into debates on representations of aggression and discourse analysis. I am also grateful to the criminal justice and psychology faculty of both institutions, who read and listened to my arguments with healthy skepticism and offered invaluable constructive comments. Crucial backup was provided by librarians and secretaries, especially Phyllis Schulze at Rutgers Criminal Justice Collection, Sandra Wright, and Andrea McLeod.

This book touches on many areas, from psychosomatic illness and experimental psychology to criminal violence and power relations. It would have been impossible to cover this amount of ground without the hard labor of those who work at the forefront of knowledge in these diverse fields. I am especially grateful to those who, through critical narrative or meta-analytic reviews, have provided others with a clear framework for comprehending their subject matter. I am thinking particularly of Angela Browne, Alice Eagly, Jeffrey Fagan, Jack Katz, Eleanor Maccoby, Merry Morash, and Dolf Zillmann.

At the core of this book is the idea that the way people represent the process of aggression to themselves is vital to understanding their actions and their interpretations of others. The idea of social representations was first explicated by Serge Moscovici. Although I know him only through his writing, I extend to him my personal thanks.

1

Cultural Lessons in Aggression

IMAGINE a scene of violence. Perhaps you visualize it in a sleazy bar or maybe in a suburban living room. Perhaps a weapon comes into play, or maybe it is limited to bare knuckles. Whether a bomb explodes, a woman is raped in a city park, someone is beaten at home or in public or is the victim of another of the robberies that have become all too common in big-city life, one thing is almost certain: The aggressor in your mind is a man. Maleness and aggression have become linked to the point where it is easy to forget about women's aggression. It takes place far less often than men's, and it rarely makes headlines. It is private, unrecognized, and frequently misunderstood. It looks and feels different from men's.

This book is about the reason for this difference. It is about the way men and women understand their own aggression. The divergence in their beliefs about what aggression means and what it achieves is what leads to their separate styles of violent behavior. Both sexes see an intimate connection between aggression and control, but for women aggression is the *failure* of self-control, while for men it is the *imposing* of control over others. Women's aggression emerges from their inability to check the disruptive and frightening force of their own anger. For men, it is a legitimate means of assuming authority over the disruptive and frightening forces in the world around them. This difference in the way the sexes understand aggression drives a behavioral wedge between them, expressed in everything from their unique styles of fighting to the gross disparity in their rates of violent crime. In marriage, husbands' and wives' separate ways of reading aggression meet head-on in dangerous spirals of misunderstanding. In society at large, men's and women's ways of handling provocation put this same conflict on a grand scale.

More is at stake here than a simple sex difference in perspective, however. As long as men hold positions of power it is *their* beliefs that count, and they tend to see women's aggression—because it remains inexplicable in male terms—as comic, hysterical, or insane.

Stories of Rage and Control

I found the first clues to the simple distinction between the way men and women think about aggression by listening to them talk about their everyday conflicts. I invited separate groups of women and men friends to my apartment with an open-ended invitation to talk about their experiences of aggression. I had been involved in research on women and aggression for nearly twenty years, and, because I accepted the fact that women commit less than 10 percent of violent crimes, I had focused my attention on those rare women who had attracted the attention of the police and the courts. So until then I had heard the voices of girl delinquents, girl gang members, and women prison inmates, but I began to suspect that I had been working from a false premise. I had been asking why these women fight and ignoring the more interesting question: How do most women avoid fighting? Like men, women are subject to anger, stress, and frustration. Yet women rarely come to blows. In the talk of ordinary women, we can glimpse the reasons why.

Nora, a twenty-nine-year-old New Yorker who has just become a mother, talks about her problems with her mother-in-law. Nora's daughter is the family's first grandchild, and her mother-in-law, a "very Italian, very overbearing woman," is terribly possessive. She has her own ideas about how to raise the baby, and the latest conflict has centered on breast-feeding. Visibly upset, Nora describes the scene to her friends:

> Robert's mother from day one is convinced that the baby isn't getting enough milk. And what it is is a power thing because she wants to have the baby two to three days at a stretch. She says, "Why

> don't you guys go out of town for a few days? She's *my* baby and I want her." . . .
>
> So it all came to a head last Sunday when she said again to me, "When is this kid going to start eating food? She's not getting enough to eat. I know I should have fixed a bottle because you must not have enough milk because she's so fussy." So there were like fifteen people there, friends and family, and I stood up and I was shaking. And I was already close to tears because I had had it up to here, and I was kind of half crying. And I said, "You look at that kid right now and you tell me she's not getting enough to eat. She's got little rolls of fat everywhere and she's happy as can be and she's a good baby and I can't believe that you have been on my case about this since the day I had her. And I have had it." And then I stopped myself because people were starting to look, and like the whole family was getting really embarrassed.

At this point Nora's friend Joanne, who knows Robert's family, interrupts: "Well, they yell at each other, don't they?" And Nora replies:

> That's right. They scream at each other constantly, and I should have realized that it didn't faze her that I'm doing this. But I'm so embarrassed that I'm making a scene—you know us Midwesterners. I'm being such a damn WASP about it all. So I sat down very quietly with her and I said, "You have to understand that I'm a first-time mother and I'm very insecure. When you say things like that it makes me feel I'm not doing a good job." And then, of course, she got all lovey-huggy: "Oh, darling. You're wonderful." And I was still so furious with her that I wanted to strangle her. And I felt that I was just swallowing all this anger, and now I had to be all lovey and nice to her.

There is a collective sigh of recognition and resignation among the group. Then Nora explains the position she is in:

> The only thing we can do is move to California. I find myself saying really bitchy things about Robert's mother in front of Robert, and I'm having a harder and harder time going over there because I am so angry at her all the time. I have to learn to be angry in an appropriate way. Because when I stood up and started to get angry with her and

> I started to cry, I thought, "This is a real disaster." I have to be able to get firm and angry, you know, and just say, "Enough." I'm still so angry.

Nora's experience, like that of many other women with whom I spoke, is one of anger and restraint. In telling her story, she devotes as much time to the germination of her anger as to its eruption, needing to underline to her friends and to herself the intolerable stress she has been placed under by her mother-in-law's unreasonable behavior "from day one." Nora has refused to give way to her anger and has consciously tried not to battle with her mother-in-law. But she has reached the breaking point. She wants to get her anger out of her system, to relinquish her self-control. Her feelings run so high that she is shaking.

For Nora, as for many other women, tears seem to be a close companion of anger. She cries not from remorse but from frustration. If she restrains her anger, she will have to deal with feelings of impotence. But if she lets go, she fears the awful power of her rage and its consequences, which cannot be taken back. She lets go, but wishes in midstream that she had not because the effect is not the liberating tension release she anticipated. She stops short. First of all, she says that she breaks off the tirade because "the whole family was getting embarrassed." But when her friend questions her about this, she realizes that it was in fact her *own* sense of propriety that was offended. As she puts it, "I stopped myself"—splitting herself into two people, the angry self and the responsible self that reins in the anger. Thus she is angry with herself on two counts: for expressing her anger and for restraining it. This encounter is between the two parts of Nora just as much as it is between Nora and her mother-in-law.

Nora tries to find a way to deal with her feelings without alienating her mother-in-law or forcing her husband to choose between his mother and his wife. She decides on a calm and reasoned discussion in which she casts herself in the subordinate role (a first-time mother) and so accords to her mother-in-law the status of expert (mother of four children). She asks only that her mother-in-law not be too critical of Nora's performance. But this appeasement does nothing to release her anger. The price Nora must pay for the triumph of self-control is continued frustration.

If outbursts of aggression are cut off as a route to solving the long-term problem, what avenues remain? Avoidance—moving to California—is not a viable solution. Nora believes that there must be an "appropriate" way to express rather than deny her own anger, but like many women she is at a loss to identify exactly what that might be. How can she be true to her own anger while not seeming to be bitchy or hysterical? How can she assert herself without threatening her relationship with other people? At the end of the dinner-table debacle, Nora remained just where she had been before—frustrated with bottled-up fury.

Two weeks later at a similar gathering, Mike, who is twenty-eight years old and works on Wall Street, recounts a story of aggression to his male friends:

> It was my friend's birthday and we were out drinking, and we had a lot to drink. We were having a great time. We walk out of the bar and there are these five guys coming out of another bar and they go, "Hey, you faggots!" Dave turns to me and says, "Don't do anything, just relax." This guy goes, "You skinny-ass mother———." I turned to Dave and I said, "That's it." I walked over to the guy—I had a lot to drink and maybe that had a lot to do with it—but I went up there. So I stood there and my teeth were gritted and I turned to the guys and said, "Which one of you jerks said that?" And they all go, "I did." I said, "What?" And this one small skinny guy looks at me and goes, "You mother———." I just grabbed him and I was all over him.

At this point Mike's friends break into raucous laughter. He continues:

> I was wailing on the guy, and then some guy came out of nowhere. Boom! He hit me right in the face. I came to and Dave had two guys in the bushes, and he was beating them up and everything. And I got up and the adrenaline was just pumping. I look up and there's two guys running this way, and the cops come screeching into the middle of the area. And this kid starts running away. The kid who started the whole thing. And I looked at him and I said, "You're not getting away with it," because I knew I was going to jail. I chased the kid. And I mean I'm running as fast as I can. All I can remember is hearing my friend say, "Don't do it! Don't do it!" And the kid's

running like into three cops. So the kid stopped and he turned around and I'm just running into him. But I hit him right in the head!

Mike's story could not be more different from Nora's. It is an exuberant, even playful recounting of a night of celebratory drinking after which two men are provoked by strangers. The fight is about heroism in the face of adversity, about winning against superior odds. Our protagonist and his loyal friend are clearly the forces of good; the forces of evil are the five strangers who call them "faggots"—an accusation, as Mike interprets it, not of homosexuality but of nonmasculinity. Mike does not need to explain or excuse his anger, as Nora did. He knows his friends understand it.

Level-headed Dave tries to hold back hot-blooded Mike from avenging the insult, but, in Mike's telling of the story, it is clear that real men go forward against even suicidal odds when their reputation is under attack. Mike's description of the fight is punctuated with laughter, both his own and that of his friends. After all, fighting among young men is a form of recreation, an extension of the rough-and-tumble fights of childhood. And it seems that their friend Mike is about to describe the triumph of their team over the upstart challengers.

But the story takes a twist when Mike is knocked out. If male stories of fighting are about controlling others, what could Mike gain by admitting to this? Male fighting talk is also about willingness to put oneself on the line, to answer challenges even when the chance of victory is slim. Sustaining injury signals that it was a dangerous fight against men who had the capacity to inflict damage. The role that self-control played for Nora is taken over in Mike's world by the police. If a man were to exercise self-control during a fight, particularly a fight that is not going well for him, it might be mistaken for cowardice. Instead he must depend on others to break things up, and even then must make it clear that he is being forced to quit.* Dave, the voice of reason and civilization, shouts at him to stop, but Mike is no longer a member of the anemic, law-abiding world. Propelled by

*The anthropologist Robin Fox studied a remote community on an island off Ireland and reported that at Saturday night dances, where a brawl was an expected sideshow, young men would wait for their friends to grab their arms and then would struggle wildly and shout, "Hold me back or I'll kill him."[1]

moral outrage, he delivers a righteous blow to the offender's head. Honor is satisfied and order is restored.

If, in men's accounts of aggression, we are told what it is like to take control, in women's accounts we hear about what it means to lose control. For women, the threat comes from within; for men, it comes from others. For women, the aim is a cataclysmic release of accumulated tension; for men, the reward is power over another person, a power that can be used to boost self-esteem or to gain social and material benefits. For women, the interpersonal message is a cry for help born out of desperation; for men, it is an announcement of superiority stemming from a challenge to that position. For women, the fear of aggression is a fear of breaking relationships; for men, it is the fear of failure, of fighting and losing, or of not being man enough to fight at all.

I call women's approach to their beliefs about their aggression *expressive,* and men's approach *instrumental.* Just as men and women are divided in their ideas, so are psychologists, as the following discussion shows. These conflicts, like most others, result from the assumption that if one side is right the other must be wrong. Could it be, however, that both sexes are right—but only about themselves?

Aggression: Theories and Action

While men and women reveal much about their understanding of aggression in ordinary conversations with one another, psychologists have been working to construct a formal theory. If I am right in believing that there is a crucial difference in the way the sexes think about aggression, then the search for a single theory of aggression will have to be abandoned in favor of a search for two theories.

What is remarkable about scientists' theories—and it was not until I had seriously listened to men and women talking about aggression that I realized this—is that they can also be divided into two types, expressive and instrumental, that share little common ground.[2]

WOMEN: KEEPING THE LID ON AGGRESSION

In the expressive theories, the victim of the aggression plays a relatively minor role in explaining it. Some form of instinct, drive, or tension simply builds up inside us over time and sooner or later has to be emptied out. Within this camp some theorists concentrate on the building-up part of the explanation and others on the emptying-out part.

Of the first group the undisputed leader is Sigmund Freud.[3] He argued for two sources of human motivation: Eros, a drive that acts to prolong and reproduce life, and Thanatos, an innate drive toward disintegration that Freud believed was directed against the self. If he was right, how is it that we all don't commit suicide? In part, it is because of a struggle between Thanatos and Eros, which, luckily for us, Eros usually wins. But it is also because displacement redirects our self-destructive energies outward; we aggress against others to avoid aggressing against ourselves.

How, then, do people manage to avoid wreaking terrible violence upon one another? The answer, according to Freud, is catharsis: Watching violent events or engaging in mild displays of anger diminishes the aggressive urge and leaves us emotionally purified and calmed. Freud would have predicted that Nora would feel better after her verbal hostility and that she would be unlikely to feel angry again for some time. Unfortunately such predictions turn out to be wrong. Couples who argue the most are those who are the most likely to become violent.[4] Husbands who push their wives are those most likely to move on to slapping and punching. The best predictor of an individual's likelihood of criminal violence this year is his criminal violence last year.[5] Violence seems to beget violence rather than decrease it.

But can "getting it out of our system" at least improve our state of mind? Laboratory studies find that men's blood pressure does indeed drop after aggressing against someone who has insulted them. But women's does not, as Nora's experience shows.[6] Our reactions to aggression depend on learning. In the normal course of growing up, girls learn to respond to their aggression not with a sense of being purified and calmed but with a sense of shame. Aggression feels good to men but not to women.

Frustration-aggression theory, another influential explanation of aggression, argues that aggression is always preceded by frustration and that frustration always leads to some form of aggression.[7] Unfortunately the second part of this sweeping claim is patently false.[8] Frustration may make you bite your tongue, think about something else, or laugh it off. Heavily influenced by behaviorism as well as by Freud, frustration-aggression theorists define *frustration* as the thwarting of an action that would have produced reward or gratification. As we are continually blocked from obtaining the rewards we try to achieve—a promotion, a parking space, a sexual partner—our frustration accumulates in relation to how highly we value the goal. For Nora, the importance of being a good mother was paramount. She would have been less offended if her mother-in-law had criticized her driving or her golf game because these activities mattered far less to her. The amount of frustration we feel also depends on whether the blocking of the goal is total or only partial; criticism of her nursing struck at the very heart of Nora's concept of motherhood. A third factor is the sheer number of frustrations; if this had been the first time her mother-in-law criticized her mothering, Nora might have passed it off more calmly.

Despite what may seem like ample reason to express it, aggression is a relatively rare event. This is mainly due to a strong counteracting force: anticipated punishment from others. We are thus less likely to become aggressive toward our boss (who may frustrate us terribly but who has considerable power to punish us) than toward our children (whom we love but who wield little real power over us). If our frustration cannot find a direct way out, we shift our anger toward those who will not punish us. Nora got angry at Robert instead of at his mother because she knew he would be more sympathetic to her. Such displacement is a relatively safe way to reduce our frustration, and the resulting catharsis releases us from the ulcer-feeding tensions of daily life.

Many psychoanalytic writers since Freud have rejected or downplayed the instinctive nature of aggression, explaining it instead in terms of deficient ego function.[9] The tension that hides behind aggression is the tension between the id and the ego. In childhood the *id*—the primitive, gratification-seeking part of our psyche—dominates: We want it all our own way and we want it now. As we mature the *ego* becomes stronger and mediates between the blind internal id and the forces of reality in the world beyond. The ego is the repository of all those qualities that separate us from animals: the ability to defer immediate gratification for the long-term good, to plan for the future, to see the world through someone else's eyes—and so to control our anger. For many neo-Freudians, it is a weak ego that lies at the heart of the problem of aggression. The explosion of Nora's id was checked by her ego as she realized that she was letting herself down, threatening her relationship with those nearest to her, and indulging a selfish and childish desire to have a tantrum.

Sociological arguments present more or less the same viewpoint in simpler terms. Theorists of social control say that, because of the self-evident attractions of doing wrong, we all naturally tend toward selfishness and consequently aggression.[10] But society requires that each of us give up a little of our selfish freedom in return for safety and harmony. We agree, for example, not to hit others in return for the assurance that they will not hit us. The task for parents is to raise a child who needs their approval and fears their disapproval enough to abide by their rules and take on their values. Aggression (as well as a host of other social ills) results when this bond fails. When it has succeeded, we keep our aggression in check, not out of a tactical fear that we will be caught and punished but out of a successfully internalized value that makes us ashamed of such actions: Social control has become self-control. Nora's eruption is finally halted by the powerful internalized social control of her Midwestern childhood.

Behavioral psychologists, on the other hand, reject such lofty notions in favor of simple conditioned responses. For them aggression is a learning deficiency.[11] When a toddler picks up a toy and throws it, she finds that her action is swiftly followed by a painful reprimand. Soon the events that preceded the slap become associated with the experience of pain. The next time she raises a toy over her head to throw it, she reexperiences the bad feelings that followed the last toy-throwing episode. She learns to stop herself, mastering "behavioral inhibition." In Nora's case, her restraint demonstrates nothing more than her successful history of conditioning, attributable to her watchful and punitive parents.

Expressive theories take a pessimistic view of human nature. Only through proper socialization and training can our basic aggression be kept under control. The minute the lid of self-control is lifted, violence will out. Women tend to think like expressive theorists. For them aggression is the first step on the slippery slope to selfishness and chaos. For thousands of years women have been the mainstay of the family, the regulators of domestic tranquility. In that role they have learned the awful consequences of aggression for personal relationships. In Nora's story we can hear the tension between upholding family bonds and the need to discharge the frustrations that these bonds create; the splitting of anger and control just as they have been described by these scientists' theories. She abhors her own aggression and will go to almost any lengths to repress it, no matter what it costs.

MEN: THE LANGUAGE OF POWER

The instrumental theorists, whose views are expressed clearly in men's ordinary accounts of their aggression, begin from a more optimistic position. People are not impelled toward aggression by their accumulated frustrations but, rather, are drawn forward into aggression by the obvious benefits it offers.

For learning theorists, aggression is simply a behavior and must be governed by the same principle as any other behavior: reinforcement.[12] People who hit do so because in the past they have been rewarded for such behavior. The most obvious rewards for violence are material ones. The toddler who kicks his peer succeeds in taking the toy he wants (unless a watchful adult intervenes). There are also social rewards for aggression. The gang member who beats up and dispatches a rival gang gains the respect of his fellow members. Mike, in his self-destructive mission to gain victory over his tormentors, established himself as a virile aggressor.

Another valuable reward of aggressive behavior is that it removes an unpleasant state. A child who has remained passive under an attack by a cruel schoolmate decides to strike back and finds, to his delight, that the attack stops. For Mike, being called a "faggot" produced extremely negative emotions. He demonstrated by the very fact of fighting that the implication of cowardice the abuse was intended to convey could not be made to stick.

For some men the reward for behaving aggressively is a boost to their shaky sense of self-worth, since it is a public demonstration of their manliness, about which they have profound doubts.[13] Such men seem to seek opportunities to behave aggressively; sleazy bars or street corners provide a steady supply of victims and an appreciative male audience for their victories. Seeing themselves as guardians of appropriate behavior, they take on troublemakers for the sake of their buddies. But behind their bravado is often a deep-seated sense of fear and vulnerability. They know only too well the feeling of powerlessness they seek to create in their victims. As long as they are the aggressors, they cannot be the victim.

Aiding and abetting this individual process are subcultures of violence whose members legitimate, even encourage, physical aggression as a response to conflict.[14] An examination of homicide data in Philadelphia gave rise to the idea of such a subculture existing in certain urban neighborhoods among people below the poverty level. Homicides in these neighborhoods seemed to result from trivial disputes. Trapped in an underclass of social isolation, these people face not only economic stress but the social stresses of illness, drugs, poor schools, crumbling buildings, and an environment where no one feels safe. In this oppressive environment tempers flare easily, aggression becomes common, and the whole social system begins to spiral upward to a crescendo of violence. Violence becomes normalized as a routine part of everyday life, and this normalization forms a subculture of violence.

But it is not so much a subculture of violence as one of masculinity, for it is painfully clear that the bulk of its members are male. Why? Sociologists tell us that the answer lies in the masculine self-concept of low-status men. Minority males have the highest rate of unemployment in the nation. Unable to provide for their families, these men tend to seek refuge from that humiliation by spending idle time in the streets. With the usual economic and social signs of successful masculinity denied to them, street-corner men must find other ways to "be somebody." By building a reputation for toughness, they can win back the pride and identity society has denied them. For some of these men, neighborhood groups and the norms they support make violence a viable way to construct an identity for themselves.[15]

Although it may be more evident in ghetto areas, the intimate connection between masculinity and aggression is not confined to the inner-city poor. Even Wall Street brokers like Mike feel that their identity as a man depends upon their willingness to fight. Such middle-class men, for all their gains in wealth and status, are acutely sensitive to the fact that they have become alienated from the brute strength that defines traditional masculinity. They see in the taunts of young, poor men a challenge not only to their privileged life but to the physicality they have renounced. Their three-piece suits and credit cards have emasculated them, torn them away from the natural relationship between manliness and physical courage still retained by the working class. Mike fights to show that he is as tough as any ghetto boy.

One instrumental theorist, James Tedeschi, says that aggression is simply coercive power—the use of threats or punishments to gain compliance and to have demands met, whether they be for money, sexual gratification, or political change.[16] When we are unable to get our way by charm, ingratiation, or rational argument, according to this theory, we resort to threats: "To be coercive, violence has to be anticipated. And it has to be avoidable by accommodation. The power to hurt is bargaining power."[17] There is something chillingly rational about this explanation. It is also an exclusively male explanation. Very few women have the desire for power that lies behind such a motivation. Forcing obedience through fear brings shame rather than satisfaction to most women. But because most men equate power with masculinity, they will attain it even at the price of another's fear. In Mike's case, being verbally taunted was an explicit announcement of his powerlessness. Since, for men, power is a zero-sum game, all pretenders to the throne must be made to accept a subordinate status.

Criminologists argue that violent crime is a form of vigilante control used to redress what the aggressor sees as a moral wrong.[18] It is most often resorted to by those who, because of poverty or race, feel they do not have recourse to legal means of imposing control. When wronged, they are unlikely to be championed by police and prosecutors, and their attitude to the criminal justice system is one of cynicism and mistrust. Before the evolution of legal systems, many societies tolerated victims who sought revenge against the person who had wronged them. And today violence has become a way of dispensing justice in which ordinary citizens enforce social control over those who have violated proper behavior. (Think of the celebrated case of Bernhard Goetz, New York's subway vigilante.) For Mike it was clear that a gross injustice had been done. In the absence of other guardians of civil liberties, he felt compelled to punish the wrongdoers himself and thus assert and protect his right to walk the streets freely.

The instrumental theories of aggression, with their common view of people behaving purposively, harmonize perfectly with the words of ordinary men talking about their experiences of violence. Men's traditional position of power in marriage and in society at large has brought with it a sense of their having a natural right to control others. Most men feel no guilt about using that power and are ready to enforce the principle of justice regardless of who may be hurt. Pride takes precedence over caring and concern. Mike and the instrumental theorists speak the same language, a language of power and dominance and the benefits that accrue from them. It is a world away from the dam-bursting view of aggression espoused by the expressive theorists and by many women.

How We Develop Our Ideas About Aggression

Scientists and ordinary men and women could not have arrived at a similar distinction between instrumental and expressive by mere chance. All of us draw our ideas from the same well of possible explanations, including what we read, what we observe, and, most important, what passes between us in everyday conversation. Scientists can no more escape their culture than the rest of us can. The ideas they bring to bear in the pursuit of science are taken, like ours, from the prevailing climate of social opinion.

But scientists also help determine which interpretations will be in vogue. Dr. Spock's *Baby and Child Care* has had an enormous influence on the way millions of parents have raised their children. Benjamin Spock believes that children must learn more "stability and self-restraint." In his opinion the aggressiveness of Americans is no greater than that of other nationalities, but it is "less controlled from childhood on" in the United States. Reading between the lines, we can see that Spock views children's aggression as an expressive process, one that needs to be restrained.[19] Another expert, Penelope Leach, takes a hard line on parents' use of physical punishment, condemning it as "revenge and power mongering." Hers is an instrumental approach, stressing the concepts of parental power and coercion.[20]

When doctors and educators speak, people not only listen but incorporate these ideas into their own explanations of aggression. In this way science becomes folklore, and academic theories become "common sense."[21] Ordinary people need to adopt ideas and explanations to keep from living in a state of confusion about why seemingly inexplicable events occur. How was the world made? Why do innocent people suffer? What lies behind the class structure in society? What causes aggression? Conflicting, unprovable theories lie behind all such questions, and a good many lively discussions in neighborhood bars and around family dinner tables are debates about whose theory is right.

These everyday theories are called *social representations.*[22] They are more than just dispassionate explanations of the causes of events. For example, our social representation of aggression encompasses our whole image and understanding of it, including the way we interpret an aggressive incident, what our emotional and moral responses to it will be, and what we actually do when we are angry. Women are likely to interpret hostile actions as stressful, unpleasant, and overwhelming, whereas men tend to see that they have been challenged, humiliated, or demeaned. This *perceptual* component both guides and is guided by the *cognitive* component of analytic thought. Cognition allows us to see similarities between this event and others, to unite them under a common representation, and to say to ourselves either, "I'm about to lose control of my anger," or, "I am going to teach that SOB a lesson."

Emotions are part of representations too, for they affect the way we feel anger. In an expressive representation, anger is tinged with fear. It feels like a rising crescendo of imminent chaos culminating in an abandonment of reason and control. But an instrumental representation implies a sense of moral outrage. If fear is present, it is the fear of not having the courage to see the encounter through. Finally, *values* are an integral part of representations. Certainly women wish that they could express their grievances and improve the treatment they receive from others, but most will stop short of injuring others and demeaning themselves. Men occasionally relish violence—in the boxing ring and macho movies, for instance—but more often they see it as simply necessary. If everyone else gave up their aggression, then men would give up theirs. But that day is never going to come, they argue, because aggression is part of male nature.

Most important of all, the social representations we hold actually shape our *behavior*. If, as a woman, I believe that the cause of my aggression is an overwhelming buildup of frustration, then I am more likely to lose my temper under stressful circumstances than others. If I believe my aggression shows that I have lost control of myself, I am more likely to be aggressive in private, more likely to feel guilty and ashamed about it, and less likely to brag to my friends about my toughness. Because aggression is a way of letting go and relieving frustration, I am as likely to scream, cry, or throw something as I am to punch someone. If I were a man, I would tend to believe that aggression is a way of imposing control and of proving who I am, and would be more likely to use it when others were insubordinate or challenged my status. I would also be more likely to take some pride in my ability to slug it out and to embellish some of the less heroic details of an incident in its retelling. Because aggression for men is usually about gaining control over others rather than discharging tension, I would be much more inclined to attack my challenger than to cry or scream. It is precisely because men and women have such different representations of aggression that they exhibit two different patterns of behavior.

Social representations are shared rather than idiosyncratic. If they were not, there would be as many theories of aggression as there are people in the world, and the patterns of aggression would not show such clear differences between men and women. We acquire these representations from others as part of our relationships with them. Parents, teachers, the media, religion, politics, college courses, and friends all provide us with frameworks for interpreting the events around us. Our society teaches boys to see aggression as an issue of interpersonal dominance, whereas girls learn that it is a failure of personal control. This emphasis on the social basis of our interpretations, however obvious it may seem, clashes head-on with current thinking in psychology. Most theories of how people explain events completely ignore the fact that people live in a social context that determines the kinds of explanations they will accept.

Consider, for example, Jean Piaget, whose ideas have long dominated the study of child development.[23] He maintains that children's thinking passes through a series of universal, predetermined stages. At each stage children are limited in their ability to explain events and are faced with events that seem even to defy explanation. The child first tries to assimilate these contradictions into his or her simple cognitive interpretation but, in grasping the complexity of the world more and more, is forced to move to a higher and more powerful form of explanation. The picture that Piaget paints is of a child struggling, utterly alone, to make sense of the world. Adults enter the picture only as bearers of complex new data for the child. They supply not answers but contradictions, which the growing child must struggle to understand.

What is missing from this analysis is the fact that children and adults are part of a social world.[24] Every facet of our understanding of daily life is influenced by those around us. Wrestling with new concepts, children drive their families to the screaming point with the endless repetition of *why?* Children are given formal answers to problems they would have no way of solving alone. In school they are told and accept on good faith that there are invisible forces at work: gravity, electricity, magnetism. If such explanations were not handed on from generation to generation and from culture to culture, the speed of progress would be slowed to a crawl. But for all our knowledge, there are areas of life that remain mysterious.

Aggression is such an area. It can be explained in multiple, contradictory ways, so a child does not receive the straightforward kind of explanation she might in the area of biology or physics. Sitting in front of the television, she may hear her parents bemoan the violence in children's cartoons and, in the next minute, wonder aloud why we don't send troops in to this or that nation. Nevertheless children do arrive at an implicit explanation of aggression, and, in the next chapter, I discuss how it is likely to be different for boys and girls.

Representations are also social in the sense that they can provide a basis for efficient communication. Listen to these two mothers at a playground. As a little girl dissolves into a screaming tantrum when she fails to wrench a toy away from her playmate, her mother remarks, "She's inherited my temper, I'm afraid. She's going to have to learn to rein it in." The women share an understanding of the child's behavior premised on an expressive view of aggression. "He's a little tyrant. He always wants to be the boss," says the second mother, as her child whacks an insubordinate peer who has failed to follow his instructions on how to build a sand castle. This mother has shifted into an instrumental explanation but, similarly, it requires no further clarification.

Sharing similar theories eases conversation between individuals, but social representations do differ from one group to another.[25] Implicit theories about aggression are not the same for governments as for revolutionaries, for Christians as for Muslims, for psychiatrists as for lawyers. They are profoundly different for men and women, as we shall see. This carries considerable political significance, since it is men who hold the reins of power and it is their representation of aggression that confronts us in politics, the media, courtrooms, and battlefields, as well as in the home. War heroes are decorated and vigilantes acclaimed. "A man's home is his castle" and within its confines, even if nowhere else, he has the right to respect and obedience. Little boys make heroes of cold-blooded killers as long as the victims are bad guys. Women may be invited to join in the applause but not to get involved themselves: Aggression is men's work.

Furthermore, the machinery that interprets aggression—science, law, and the media—is operated by men, and the male viewpoint has hogged the airtime to such an extent that women accept it even while recognizing that it does not speak of their own experiences. The picture of aggression handed to us by the media shows its instrumental use: to humiliate, conquer, and control. Curiously absent are women's experiences of anger: repression, frustration, then explosion. When a woman does reach the limit of her self-control and strikes out, men tend to be dumbstruck. Her behavior does not fit the representation of coercion and power through which they view it and thus seems unpredictable and pointless. But there is just as much logic and consistency in women's view of aggression as in men's. Though men's and women's representations of aggression serve the status quo, they are not powered by a giant political conspiracy. They are acquired in the course of childhood from social influences and seem to appear naturally. But the process is a complex one, and it is to the development of these different understandings of aggression that I turn in the next chapter.

2

Boys, Girls, and Aggression

PSYCHOLOGISTS have confirmed by painstaking observation of free play what mothers have always known: By the age of three, boys wrestle, hit, kick, tussle, push, and pull far more than girls do.[1] What's more, mothers feel responsible for their children's behavior, and they talk about their boisterous and belligerent sons in a defensive tone: "I don't know where he gets it from—we don't encourage him to fight." "We never gave him guns. But then he started making them out of old paper-towel rolls. If you don't buy them, they just make them by themselves." "He's not so bad at home with me. It's when he's with other boys that he starts fighting and being aggressive."

Aggression is clearly an antisocial behavior to most women, and many mothers of boys sense, quite rightly, that psychologists blame them for their sons' behavior.[2] But research now shows that mothers are equally intolerant of aggression in sons and daughters and that they use the same verbal reprimands and punishment for both.[3] This is part of a bigger picture that suggests that mothers are relatively sex-blind when it comes to raising their children.

Should we conclude, then, that boys are born violent? Genes may explain the sex difference in rates of aggression,[4] but the distinct pattern that characterizes men's aggression is acquired from a culture that rationalizes and even glorifies male violence. Boys are not simply more aggressive than girls; they are aggressive in a different way. They fight to take possession of toys and territory, to compete and win socially, to be recognized as tough guys. They fight because aggression performs a function for them in terms of power and recognition. A little boy may begin life with a greater readiness for aggression, but he still has a lot to learn from his culture. He must learn whom he can fight, what constitutes an adequate provocation, how to conduct his violence, and when he can reasonably expect condemnation, recognition, or glory for his actions. This is a long way from the rough-and-tumble play of the nursery.

But what about girls? What explanation of their relative placidity can we offer, if not genetics? Women are not born calm. There is ample evidence that women experience anger as often and as deeply as men. As babies they cry and scream just as much.[5] But they learn different lessons about aggression than boys do. Whereas a boy moves away from his mother's condemnatory, expressive view of aggression into a world of men, where its instrumental value is understood, the girl makes no such change. She remains selectively tuned in to a female wavelength, searching for clues to femininity and to aggression. But she finds little to examine. After her mother's early censuring of overt displays of aggression, there is a gaping void. The most remarkable thing about the socialization of aggression in girls is its absence. Girls do not learn the right way to express aggression; they simply learn not to express it. To understand the process by which boys and girls come to differ in their aggression, we must begin at the beginning, with infancy.

The Hand That Rocks the Cradle

Asked continually whether they want a boy or a girl, pregnant women have a stock answer: "I don't care as long as the baby is healthy." After the birth, the surge of love and protectiveness most mothers experience does seem truly sex-blind. The baby's needs for warmth, contact, and milk are immediate, and the day when this small bundle will emerge clearly as a boy or girl seems far off. In the months and years that lie ahead, the child will inevitably move toward a gendered set of interests and behaviors, but research shows that it is the father, not the mother, who will nudge the child toward this specialization. And that paternal push will be felt far more by boys than by girls.

Two Texan researchers demonstrated this ingeniously by bringing young children into a playroom equipped with sex-typed toys.[6] The "boy" toys included soldiers, war vehicles, a highway with cars, and a cowboy outfit. The "girl" toys consisted of a dollhouse, a toy stove with pots and pans, and dress-up outfits consisting of dresses, hats and shoes. With the boys' set, both boys and girls were told to play with the toys the way a boy would and, with the girls' set, to play like a girl would. Once each child had begun to play, the child's parents were brought into the room to watch. The researchers would then note positive reactions (such as joining in, helping, and showing approval) and negative reactions (such as interfering and expressing disgust or disapproval) by the parents. Fathers' were nearly *five times* as disapproving of cross-sex play by boys than by girls. Mothers did not differ in their level of disapproval for either sex. This effect has been found to show up with infants as early as twelve months of age, in play sessions where fathers offered trucks and dolls with equal frequency to their daughters but systematically withheld dolls from their sons.[7]

We still do not fully understand why gender typing is relatively unimportant to mothers compared to fathers. It may be the simple fact of the mothers' closer emotional tie to the child. Sex (like race or age) is a salient fact about anyone we meet. As we come to know the other person, we make much finer discriminations about him or her. Sense of humor or bad temper or intelligence seem to override biological facts. A mother has been forming a kind of relationship with her infant for nine months before the birth, and this continues infinitely more intensely in the weeks and months that follow. She may be too close to her baby to see gender as an important issue.

Or perhaps it is the nature of her role that dims her preoccupation with her child's sex; first and foremost, she must devote herself to the child's health and well-being. She is, in short, more concerned with survival in the rawest sense than with the man or woman whom that survival will finally ensure.

Or it could be something more profoundly tied to her own gender. It is men, not women, who tend to devalue femininity, seeing dependence and emotions as weaknesses. Since women see nothing wrong with their qualities of empathy, nurturance, and love, they see no reason to discourage or suppress them in their daughters *or* their sons. Perhaps women even hope that their sons can grow into adults who will feel able to express tenderness. At the same time, they see all around them the benefits that men gain by their boisterousness and bravado. A girl, possessing these traits as well as softer feminine ones, might enjoy the best of both worlds.

One result of this is that a mother tends to react similarly to displays of aggression by a son or a daughter. Because of her expressive view, she believes that aggression results from an overwhelming sense of frustration on the child's part. Thus she interprets screaming, kicking, and the tantrums of the "terrible twos" as the results of the child's inability to control the frustrations of daily life. And infants spend a lot of time in a state of frustration, since their every need must be met by their mothers, who are not always prescient enough to know exactly what their infants want. Aggression is the explosion of that frustration in a child too young to tolerate any delay of gratification. While the mother understands the dynamics that produce aggression, she neither excuses nor condones it. As the child grows, the mother recognizes that it is vital—both for the child's future as a social being and for the mother's sanity—that self-control be imposed.

Mothers are also aware that babies are not intentionally aggressive. In the first months of life, an infant seems unaware of the consequences of his own actions and reacts to events rather than initiating them. He cries when he is hungry, curls his toes when his feet are tickled, sleeps when he is tired, and screams when he is frustrated. Mothers do not ordinarily think of the child *choosing* to do these things, but the child's reactions produce effects on the mother's behavior. She prepares a bottle when she hears hunger cries, and scolds him when he screams in anger.

But a child is not able to see the connection between his behavior and the response it evokes until he is several months old.[8] Thus the mother interprets the child's aggression, as she does her own, as unintended, the difference being that the mother values control, is extremely proficient at exercising it, and in consequence is rarely aggressive. When she is, she experiences guilt and remorse. Both sexes must also learn to acquire and value control and to experience shame when that control is lost. And indeed, after an "outburst peak" between the ages of one and two, tantrums diminish rapidly in frequency. The crucial difference between the sexes, as we shall see, is that girls' socialization in the management of aggression effectively ends there, while boys learn to control their anger in order to be more effective in using aggression as a way of controlling other people.

The mother's control over her own aggression and her child's obvious absence of such control reinforce the power balance of the pair. She possesses a quality that she will teach to the infant, and she is the ego ideal toward which the child gravitates. For women, especially those whose status is derived exclusively from the family, this is a rare opportunity to be a role model to someone clearly subordinate to themselves.

But if the mother gives an instrumental interpretation to her child's aggression, she will see it not as an emotional eruption but as a tool for controlling her. She will feel her self-control exploited by an infant tyrant, who uses his aggression to subordinate her. She faces a no-win choice: She can maintain her own self-control at the cost of seeming to give way to the child's tyranny, or she can join battle and counterassert her own power through retaliation. The specter of such an escalation of violence is anathema to most women. Each skirmish is not only emotionally devastating but threatens the intimate relationship between the two of them. Unlike the child, she must live with her guilt. A lifetime of socialization in the suppression of her own aggression is not easily discarded. In the face-off between mother and child, she will almost always blink first.

Most women (most of the time) find that an expressive interpretation makes for a happier family life. But a few do not. Women who physically abuse their children seem to view their infant's angry outbursts as intentional and manipulative. Many of these women have been the victims of abuse themselves. They may feel cornered and controlled by those around them. If attempts to soothe and comfort the child fail to stop the child's screaming, such mothers may come to see the tantrums as a deliberate personal attack on their adequacy as mothers. A study of abusive and nonabusive mothers of difficult children found that both groups felt explosive anger.[9] The nonabusive women had developed techniques for increasing control over their anger, however. Some tell themselves that the child cannot help it;

others consciously remember their feelings of love and tenderness at the time of the birth; others simply put the child into a safe playpen and leave the room until they feel able to face the scene without resorting to violence.

But mothers use an expressive interpretation most of all because they are women. It is not that women necessarily think their view is morally better (although some certainly do), it is simply more immediate and more relevant. Women do not change like chameleons by virtue of becoming mothers. If they have always seen aggression as a hurtful, disruptive force, they will continue to do so when they raise their children—male or female—and will signal their disapproval of the emotion of anger as well as the importance of exerting control over its expression. With phrases such as, "If you can't say anything nice, don't say anything at all," and, "Nobody likes people who hit," they drive home the message that maintaining relationships requires the suppression of aggression. (As a child I was told to leave the room until I had gained control of myself—a perfect blend of social rejection combined with a clearly expressive view of aggression as loss of self-control.)

With age, children start to direct their anger toward others who thwart or block their wishes. This may be parents but usually it is peers. Here the mother's focus is on the harm that could be sustained: "You might have hurt that little boy" or "Look what you've done. You've made her cry." Comments such as, "Would you like it if someone did that to you?" firmly direct the child to step beyond anger to the development of empathy for the victim. Perhaps most important, the child is reprimanded by the mother and encouraged to experience guilt about his actions. Making the child apologize (even against his natural inclinations) publicly shames him and casts him in the role of wrongdoer and supplicant. The maternal maxim, "I don't care who started it, say you're sorry," tells the child that aggression is treated as a misbehavior for which there is no mitigation.

Although these kind of comments occur randomly and unpredictably throughout childhood, they send the consistent and clear message that aggression is a loss of control that threatens relationships, hurts others, and shows a lapse of proper decorum. But if the mother responds like this to her sons as well as her daughters, why do they grow up to be so different?

The Discovery of Gender

By the age of two, most children are able to correctly identify themselves as a boy or a girl.[10] But this does not mean that the concept has been fully grasped. It may be seen as an arbitrary label by which the child describes himself, along with other descriptive terms such as "good" or "hungry." The acid test is the capacity to use gender to classify others correctly. The next step is to learn to identify the sex of adults and then that of other children, which is usually accomplished by the age of three. But we cannot firmly discount the possibility that children learn sex typing much earlier. For example, when children incorrectly generalize to other adults, they rarely make gender errors.[11] It is a strange man, not a strange woman, whom a child may mistakenly greet as Daddy.

An intriguing demonstration of the crucial importance of gender identity in children's thinking came from a study of over one hundred hermaphroditic patients whose assigned sex at birth was contradicted by later evidence.[12] Providing the "reassignment" to the opposite sex took place before the age of *three,* the child's psychosexual development was not grossly affected, but definite maladjustment was noted among children who were relabeled at an older age. A child interprets people, conversations, and events in terms of male or female, "like me" or "not like me." Once information has been processed down one of these gender avenues, it becomes very difficult for the child to back up and enter another.

Theorists who write about gender socialization agree on one major fact: Gender identity is the first step on the road to sex typing of behavior.[13] The child cannot control the stream of information that floods over him every day, but he can selectively attend to those parts that are relevant to him. By the age of three, boys and girls notice gender-relevant information everywhere. This discovery of gender allows the child to play an active role in his own socialization by attuning him to those topics, interests, and actions that are relevant to his sex. Once a boy discovers the male team, he elects himself happily onto it and places a higher value on "boy play" than on "girl play."[14] Girls are equally happy to join the female side. Both are convinced that their sex is the best one.

The mastering of one's gender identity carries important implications for aggression. A study by the psychologist Beverly Fagot demonstrated that girls with gender identity showed significantly less aggression than girls without it. The boys' aggression was higher overall and did not diminish with the understanding that they were boys; in fact, it increased somewhat.[15] The amount of aggression depended not on chronological age but on whether the children understood that they were a girl or a boy.

This crucial study suggests that a major impact of gender identity for girls is the *suppression* of their own aggression. Boys, however, enter a period in which they recognize aggression as an important component of being male. But growing up male or female involves more than just the intellectual recognition of gender. It occurs in an emotional context that attaches different meanings and values to aggression.

Loving, Leaving, or Staying

Even today, both boys and girls nearly always spend their infancy around women. Feminine roles, styles, and social representations are deeply familiar to children of both sexes. They are at home in the world of women.[16] Thus for a boy to become a man, he must shift his attachment away from his mother. This process carries with it the seeds of the isolation, competition, and fear of dependence that typically characterize the male sex. It would be easier if he could simply shift his alliance from his mother to his father. But in many families, a boy sees his father only sporadically and for short periods. The vast majority of his waking life continues to be spent with his mother, female caregivers, or female teachers. His father may be his new partner, but he is an absent one.

Since the boy must define himself by his difference from the major source of his intimate support, he learns by counterimitation to avoid and eventually to disparage qualities that are feminine. His dependence on his mother and other women becomes divorced from, and even antithetical to, his development as a man. When his father is at work, he can turn to cultural images, particularly television, to watch men in action. There are few mothers who have not winced at their sons' deeply held regard for Batman, Teenage Mutant Ninja Turtles, and G.I. Joe. Not only is the boy bombarded with a parody of violent masculinity but there is no attachment between him and the men he seeks to emulate. Emotion and masculinity are cut off from each other in the images of the men he sees and in the remote and disengaged way he watches them.

This wedge that is now driven between the boy and his mother sets the emotional stage for learning about aggression. He begins to place a higher value on masculine autonomy and control than on enduring relationships. The dire consequences of aggression as described by his mother—the rupturing of relationships, the loss of another's love, the possibility of injury inflicted on a friend—begin to lose their sting. He has broken away from the dependency of his first years, and he understands that by sacrificing this intimacy, he gains power over others. Women's views no longer matter; when they diverge from masculine orthodoxy, they are wrong. What sense does his mother's expressive interpretation of aggression make in a male world where returning soldiers are welcomed as heroes and where conscientious objectors are cowards?

But the girl's deep attachment to her mother is cemented, not sundered, by the knowledge that they share the same gender. The girl understands what it is to be a woman by being engaged daily in a particular relationship with one. Unlike the boy, she need not rely on abstract images. Her gender-role learning is suffused with attachment and affection, while the boy's demands emotional withdrawal. It is in this linking of learning and loving that many psychologists see the roots of women's distinctively relational view of the social world. Dependence and a sense of connection are at the core of girls' gender learning, just as independence and autonomy are at the heart of a boy's.

Indeed, for women the principal developmental difficulty is an inability to separate from the mother, just as for men the price of maturity is often an inability to relate. The comfort and security bred by the daily relationship of mother and daughter can become so highly prized that the daughter sees any conflict between them as a threat. This fear will extend to other relationships as she grows up, so that she learns it is better to swallow hard and bottle up her anger than to risk the ugly words and blows that might cast her out into the cold world of social rejection.

As their children grow older, mothers employ what has been called "relational control." They incorporate their children in a positive network of relationships that require reciprocal obligations and duties. Misbehavior is treated as an action that is selfish, inconsiderate, and harmful to others rather than as an indictable offense to be policed and punished. This stands in stark contrast to "instrumental control" (often used by fathers), in which misbehavior is treated as a moral wrongdoing subject to formal retribution from above. Instrumental control hinges upon hierarchical relationships in which those in authority monitor, apprehend, and punish those without authority. The aim of instrumental control is to instill fear and obedience ("Don't do it or you will be punished"). The aim of relational control is to instill mutual concern and responsibility. ("If you do it, you will hurt people").

The sociologist John Hagan and his colleagues have studied the impact of mothers' relational control on the aggressive and delinquent behavior of their sons and daughters. They found that mothers use relational control more on daughters than on sons, and that it has a direct impact on reducing the likelihood of aggression by daughters. Encouraging daughters to consider the effect of their own behavior on the well-being of others is an effective way to control aggression. Mothers have probably known this for some time. But why don't they use it more on their sons? Is it simply because boys do not respond to it as successfully as girls? Hagan's analysis says otherwise:

> The reason maternal relational control results in less delinquency among daughters than sons is not because daughters are more sensitive to maternal relational control but simply because they experience more of it. Or said yet another way daughters are not less delinquent because they are inherently different, but because they are treated differently.[17]

The reason why women don't use it on their sons is because of the father. Hagan compared father-dominant families to egalitarian families and found that when the father is dominant, the mother is more likely to confine her use of relational control to her daughters. It seems that a strong father discourages the son from forming a close relationship with the mother. Instead he encourages the son to define himself as distinct and opposite to her. In egalitarian families the mother uses relational control over both sons and daughters, and both show an equally low rate of aggressive delinquency.

The Making of Manhood

As the boy's gaze turns determinedly toward his often-absent father, what is projected is as important as what is perceived. Once male and female have been grasped, the child strives to clarify the distinction. He does so by exaggerating the differences, as if turning up the contrast dial on the television. When he has decided that a role or behavior is masculine, he will brook no argument or discussion. There can be no overlap between male and female and so no room for confusion. The gender conventions assume the moral force of divine law.

The psychologist William Damon conducted a series of interviews with children about gender-typed behaviors. By the age of about five, he noted a definite trend toward conservatism: Most children thought it was simply *wrong* to engage in cross-sex behavior. Listen to one five-year-old trying to make sense of the behavior of George—a boy, invented by the interviewer, who likes to play with dolls:

> (Why do you think people tell George not to play with dolls?) Well, he should only play with things that boys play with. The things that he's playing with now is girls' stuff. . . . (Can George play with Barbie dolls if he wants to?) No sir! (How come?) If he doesn't want to play with dolls, then he's right, but if he does want to play with dolls, he's double wrong. (Why is he double wrong?) All the time he's playing with girls' stuff. (Do you think people are right when they tell George not to play with girls' dolls?) Yes. (What should George do?) He should stop playing with the girls' dolls and start playing with the G.I. Joe. (Why can a boy play with a G.I. Joe and not a Barbie doll?) Because if a boy is playing with something, like if a boy plays with

> a Barbie doll, then he's just going to get people teasing him, and if he tries to play more, to get girls to like him, then the girls won't like him either.[18]*

The boy's concern with the social disapproval of behaving like a girl is reinforced by the father's strong discouragement of feminine activities. One father of a toddler, when asked if he would be disturbed about femininity in his son, told an interviewer: "Yes, I would be, very very much. Terrifically disturbed—couldn't tell you the extent of my disturbance. I can't bear female characteristics in a man. I abhor them."[19] For most men an effeminate son is far more worrying than a tomboy daughter. The father places heavy emphasis on the *avoidance* of feminine behaviors, rather than on the active encouragement of masculine ones.

Avoidance learning of this kind hinges on the evocation of anxiety and even fear about engaging in a taboo activity.[20] It is a form of learning that is deeply emotional and powerful. Because it successfully deters the individual from ever attempting to breach the taboo, it guarantees that he will never discover that it is safe to do so. By its nature, avoidance learning is a self-perpetuating process. And this back-to-front learning by which femininity is *discouraged* (rather than masculinity encouraged) leads the boy back to women once again. Femininity thus becomes the dominant image and masculinity its inverted reflection. Little boys learn from their fathers, "If you want to be like me, don't be like her."

But the boy needs more. He needs to construct a positive image of this elusive masculinity that he can project onto his father. He learns from the culture all around him the key connection between masculinity and violence. It is men, not women, who slay dragons and fight in defense of the innocent. The literary heroes of boys' worlds

*This developmental stage in which boys and girls are very clearly demarcated is part of a more general cognitive trend that shows up in children's beliefs about morality. When asked to resolve examples of moral dilemmas, children in the earliest stages of development judge as morally wrong any action that might incur the disapproval of others—particularly adults and other authority figures. This is called the punishment and obedience orientation. In the example here, the boy is chiefly concerned about disapproval by other boys, but some subjects stress that George mustn't play with dolls because his parents will (and should) punish him for doing so.

are fearless warriors, flying aces, crime fighters. From Tom and Jerry to the Teenage Mutant Ninja Turtles, from Superman to Indiana Jones, it is males who both use and receive violence. We see more aggression in one evening of television viewing than most of us either experience or witness in our whole lives. And because it is so tightly tied to masculinity, aggression becomes central to the boy's notion of manhood.

Once aggression has been linked with maleness, the boy attends much more strongly to same-sex television characters[21] and even exaggerates the crucial importance of violence for men. His caricatured stereotype of masculinity projects itself back onto the world of men, squeezing and forcing even the most improbable male candidates into its contours. Boys elevate their fathers into barely recognizable he-men and come to blows with other boys over whose father is the toughest. Lawrence Kohlberg, a developmental psychologist, recorded the words of a five-year-old boy talking to his academic and sedentary father: "Oh Daddy, how old will I be when I can go hunting with you? We'll go to the woods, you with your gun, me with my bow and arrow. Daddy, wouldn't it be neat if we could lasso a wild horse? Do you think we could do it? Do you think I could ride a horse backward if someone's leading me, like you?"[22] It is as if the boy, struggling to interpret masculinity from a counterimage of femininity, is asking, "Daddy, is this who we are supposed to be?"

Lessons from the Classroom and the Playground

As they acquire gender identity both boys and girls prefer same-sex playmates,[23] but boys are much more rigid in enforcing male behavior. Examining forty children aged between twenty-one and twenty-five months who were attending their first play group, the psychologist Beverly Fagot found that both boys and girls responded more positively to their own than to the opposite sex. But boys rewarded other boys far more when they played with masculine toys, and they had a derogatory way of reacting to sex-inappropriate play: "You're silly, that's for girls"; "That's dumb, boys don't play with dolls." Also of note were boys' and girls' differing abilities to influence each other's behavior. Although boys were affected by the reactions of other boys, they were impervious to the comments of girls. Once again, boys construct masculinity by rejecting the feminine—and they do it with a vengeance, as Fagot describes:

> We see that the male peer group starts defining what is *not male* very early and that the behaviors that are defined as not male drop out of the boy's repertoire. . . . We can see in these young children what might be called the tyranny of the male group, if one is not enthralled with the consequences, or the beginnings of the male bonding process, if one is.[24]

Boys are far more aggressive than girls, as we have seen, especially in grabbing for objects but also in hitting, pushing, and kicking. And they are twice as likely to pick on their own sex as on girls. Although teachers criticize or restrain boys' aggression more than girls', the impact of this adult disapproval appears to be negligible. Most important, boys' aggression provokes some kind of peer response over 70 percent of the time—usually from other boys.[25] Their most likely reactions are counteraggression, restraint, and criticism. It seems that for boys these responses are just as satisfying as more obviously positive reactions, such as making favorable comments or joining in the rough play. What boys learn is that aggression is an effective means of producing a reaction: Aggression confers agency. And boys' assertiveness is far more successful in material terms than is girls'. In disputes over toys, for example, boys' aggression far more often ends in possession of the toy.[26] So boys also learn that fighting wins them immediate material rewards.

It also promises the achievement of social power in the long term. Girls play just as vigorously as boys (they run, jump, and throw balls), but they rarely hit or wrestle. When these physical fights do erupt, girls are more likely to cry or retreat to their mothers. Boys seem to thrive on these violent encounters.[27] And although they seem ostensibly to be over the ownership of a toy or a territory, these disputes are simply vehicles for the bigger issue of who is in control. Such fights are most frequent in newly formed groups where the boys have yet to decide who is the boss. So the ability to provoke a response, whether positive (signaling acceptance of the boys' authority) or negative (indicating a challenge to it), is an integral part of the process by which boys use aggression to create social order. The opposite of positive reaction is not negative reaction but indifference.

The developmental shift from instrumental aggression as a means of gaining toys or territory to its use as a means of gaining self-esteem is suggested by the psychologist William Hartup.[28] He observed 102 children between the ages of four and seven as they played together, noting every incident of aggression and distinguishing between what he called instrumental and hostile acts. He defined *hostile* acts as those in which the provocation was a direct threat to the child's self-esteem, and *instrumental* acts as those in which the goal was to take possession of a toy or a territory. He found that hostile aggression was more common once the child grew older and had discovered the link between aggression and self-respect. Boys showed much greater use of hostile aggression than girls. Boys come to equate aggression with self-esteem in a way that girls simply do not.

The message that girls receive from their peers about gender-appropriate behavior is much more liberal.[29] Girls respond positively twice as often to other girls than to boys.[30] But, unlike boys, these positive reactions are independent of the gender-appropriateness of their friends' play activity. They simply do not make the same strict demands that boys do about conforming to gender stereotypes. Consequently childhood play for girls is characterized by much more flexibility and latitude. In one North American survey of women, between half and three-quarters of the respondents said that as children they had been "tomboys."[31] The majority of instances of cross-gender play, visible in children as young as three, are of girls engaging in masculine activities.[32] Asked to pick their most disliked toy, three-year-old boys are much more likely than girls to pick opposite-sex toys. At least in childhood, girls enjoy much greater freedom to foray into the make-believe world of men.

This tolerance of different play preferences is mirrored in the more unstructured nature of female peer groups, which are not characterized by the tussling and struggling for dominance so common in boys' groups.[33] Friendship cliques among girls are distinguished by the fact that members explicitly deny that there is a leader, even though observation suggests that some girls influence group choices and activities more than others. Sex differences in the structure of friendship groups are marked by the age of seven. Younger girls tend to flit around from group to group, but by then they form attachments to a handful of best friends. At the same age boys show an opposite transition, toward larger groups and gangs. Girls spend more time together, confide in one another more, and feel more trust in their friends than boys do.

Girls' friendships are also much less conflict-ridden than those of boys, and the key to this relative harmony may be in the structure of the group itself. Its smaller size is conducive to discussion and negotiation. It is built around mutuality rather than leadership, cooperation rather than competition. If one girl monopolizes a particular toy or always insists on going first in a game, the others invoke considerations of fairness and reciprocity to control her behavior. If mediation fails, girls tend to abandon the game altogether rather than escalate the dispute into aggression. While boys' games are governed by rules that must be enforced—by violence, if necessary—and with suitable penalties for deviation, for girls a game is a vehicle for friendship; rule enforcement goes only as far as persuasion and discussion. Their mothers' lessons have been well learned: No game is worth the rupturing of friendships. The use of aggression to resolve conflict is simply illogical to girls. Aggression does not solve interpersonal disputes; it merely breaks relationships.

Fagot's study also highlights the crucial importance of girls' increasing ability to control their angry impulses and to find nonviolent means of resolving disputes.[34] The real impact of gender identity is expressed not so much by an increase in aggression by boys but in a decrease by girls. I have suggested that part of the reason for that lies with the importance girls attach to maintaining harmony, but the data reveal another, more direct and concrete cause. Girls' aggression simply does not work as a form of instrumental control.[35] It is ineffective at the most basic level—that of communication. When girls aggress, nobody notices and nobody reacts. Nursery teachers are far more likely to ignore aggression by girls thirteen months and fourteen months old than by boys of the same age. Teachers respond to boys when they scream, cry, or whine; they respond to girls when they use gestures, gentle touches, and speech. By the age of two, girls' aggression is much more likely to be ignored by playmates than is boys', and this lack of response is very effective in stopping the behavior. Boys are overwhelmingly more successful than girls in using aggression to gain compliance from another child. So the little girl learns not only that aggression is emotionally dangerous but that it doesn't get her what she wants.

Rules of the Game

The instrumental benefits of male aggression are constantly amplified and extolled to boys through fairy stories, formal education, the media, and daily conversations. In the nursery, princes slay dragons to defend womanhood, and Peter Pan fights duels to consign the evil Captain Hook to the jaws of the crocodile. Knights and their pages joust at tournaments or join the Crusades to roust the heathen hordes. History for most schoolchildren is a never-ending procession of kings and male despots leading conquering armies to claim or reclaim territory. Revolutions and civil wars are about soldiers, guns, and the use of violence to achieve rightful ends. Literature at school is mostly the writings of men reflecting the masculine ideals of agency, autonomy, and often violence. International politics, whether interpreted by teachers or newspapers, is the story of conflicts. Violence, in the form of wars, police actions, or terrorism, is about the use of force to seize power, dominate, and control.

These are stories of the heroic exercise of aggression against villainy. The media presents violence almost without exception as a means to an end. So seemingly natural is the media's portrayal of male instrumental violence that it becomes visible only when we try to find examples of men showing expressive aggression. When did you last see a man on television lash out in a state of uncontrolled frustration? When have you read a newspaper account of a man racked with guilt or remorse about something he had done? The candidates are pitifully few compared to the standard fare of grim-faced, monosyllabic macho heroes standing proud and alone against the threatening forces of frontier bandits, criminals, or Vietnamese soldiers.

The men who employ aggression are heroes: the president whose army returns in triumph from a foreign war; the subway rider who shoots his assailants and instantaneously shifts from victim to victor; the movie star whose trademark is an icy stare and the wordless and cold-blooded use of lethal violence. The boy sees that the successful use of force not only gains territory or toys; it brings with it admiration and esteem. His mother has not told him the whole story about aggression.

As he moves out onto the stage of manhood, he will also see that aggression is laudable only when it is used properly. The rules of propriety are not explicit, however, and he will have to deduce from hints and clues that aggression wins respect only when the odds of winning are equal or unfavorable. When the odds are too favorable, it is bullying. He hears his father say, "Don't be so rough, she's a girl," or "It's easy to be tough when there's two of you and one of him." He overhears the conversations of adults: "She left him because the bastard was beating her up"; "Six of the cowardly little thugs grabbed him in the subway." But most of all, the message is driven home by television. Anything that tips the scales changes the morality of the encounter: only bad guys break the rules.

The real world, of course, does not always tidily conform to this equation. In the gulf war in 1991, the American media made much of the fact that Iraq had the fourth largest army in the world and that the Iraqi Republican Guard was a crack team of dedicated soldiers. This was in the service of presenting the encounter as a fair fight rather than a case of bullying by a major superpower. (Needless to say, the Iraqi media chose to present the latter view.) Regardless of the moral rights and wrongs, it was vital that the rules of propriety were seen to be observed if the allied forces were to lay claim to a great victory.

For the same reason, movies often use the device of a final showdown and shootout between two individuals, the lawbreaker and the law enforcer, even when the massed forces of the entire police department are waiting outside the door. It is not the moral rightness of the cause that justifies aggression (however much we would like to think it is) so much as its form. And the form we find most abhorrent is bullying.

The other side of the coin is the situation in which the protagonist faces an opponent who clearly has a massive tactical advantage over him: The boy who, when challenged by a gang of schoolmates to hand over his lunch money, refuses to do so is a son of whom most fathers would be proud; the lone rider from out of town who takes on the terrorizing outlaws may be crazy, but he is obviously the hero of the movie. These rules guide boys through the confusing jungle of aggression, pointing out the heroes and villains, allowing boys to tailor their actions and their talk to conform with the proper exercise of instrumental aggression.

For girls the scenario is very different. If their aggression is ignored by teachers and friends, it is all but invisible in the media and schoolbooks. On children's television female characters (if they appear at all) almost never engage in aggression. Even "tomboy" characters do not initiate or take part in violence, though they may be present to encourage and applaud the heroic actions of male figures. More often they are the helpless victims of the bad guys, awaiting rescue by the heroes. When females are shown in instrumentally aggressive roles (as police officers or army recruits), their interest value lies in their "oddity" so that, rather than normalizing female aggression, such programs manage to make it the exception that proves the rule.

By largely ignoring the subject of female aggression, television manages to reinforce the silence that surrounds it and effectively signals that the topic is so deviant that it cannot even be discussed. The invisibility of female aggression extends well beyond children's television. History and politics are the stories of male power and violence. Women are distinctly absent from the main action and may instead be found sewing flags, knitting before the guillotine, or sending Christmas packages to the troops. In the world of sport women remain in the nonconfrontational arenas of tennis, golf, or gymnastics. In contact sports women appear only in wrestling "freak shows" where they amuse rather than compete.

Even literature tends to push aggressive women into the two equally unattractive roles of witch or bitch. In fairy stories wicked queens, stepmothers, and witches use violence to eliminate rivals and rid themselves of their children, but the frisson of fear that such stories evoke springs from the dramatic device of casting a woman as an aggressor—a twist that flies in the face of most children's experience of mothers and baby-sitters. Most contemporary aggressive women on television or in novels are bitchy. From soap operas to "The Taming of the Shrew," from Catwoman to King Lear's daughters, the very use of violence clearly casts a woman in the role of villain.

Boys recognize bad guys by their refusal to follow the rules of fighting. Girls recognize bad women by their use of aggression at all. Good girls don't fight.

As a boy moves toward adulthood, he attains masculinity by following a narrow path beset on either side by the dangers of effeminacy. The price of failure is high. The taunt of "Mama's boy," for example, is a stinging accusation, and he will learn to steer clear of it. His mother and sisters watch him as he leaves their world and enters a new one. But he doesn't look back. He's not a sissy.

The girl's route to adulthood is a much wider highway and, if she occasionally strays, it seems to be of no real consequence. She can dawdle along the way to try her hand at climbing trees, playing sports, and being a cowboy. But if she ventures too far and experiments with aggression, she will hear not accusations but a terrible silence.

The different routes each has taken can be heard in their voices as adults. In the next two chapters we listen to men and women speak about their own aggression.

3

Fighting Aggression: Women and Anger

EIGHT women friends came together one night in New York City to talk about aggression. In their twenties and thirties, most held professional jobs or were on leave from them to raise their children. I had invited them to my apartment for the talk, and they had all agreed to allow the tape recorder under the coffee table. The conversation I thought might last an hour lasted nearly five. By the end they had laughed, argued, and commiserated about an aspect of their lives they had rarely discussed but about which they all had clear recollections and strong emotions.

Sex differences in aggression have been studied in the laboratory and in surveys and have produced a wealth of data but no sense of aggression as a lived experience. I wanted to concentrate in detail on a few people, listening carefully to the words and phrases they chose to communicate their real life aggressive feelings and actions. Later I would face the task of generalizing from this small and highly selected group to a wider sample of men and women.[1] First I wanted to hear about typical aggression—not sensational murders but the kinds of conflicts we have all been through—just as it was conveyed among friends.

But I got far more than this. It wasn't until I played back the tape that I fully realized that hidden just below the surface of these women's jokes, anecdotes, and anger was their own theory about women's aggression. And it was an expressive theory. As I read and reread the transcript, certain words jumped off the page at me—

anger, control, guilt, embarrassment—all from an expressive dictionary of aggression.

Their stories of aggression followed a sequence that is peculiarly characteristic of expressive accounts. First comes anger, for these women as for many others a force of destruction that looms as a constant threat to relationships. Initially it is accompanied by restraint and self-control. But when the provocation continues, as it does when their restraint is mistaken for acceptance, the anger mounts until it must find some means of release. The first option for most women is crying. But when fury builds up higher, a woman can erupt into physical aggression—to the horror, amusement, or embarrassment of those around her. Their responses reinforce her realization that she has broken the rules. Rather than question the unfairness of the double standard that condones aggression in men while condemning it in women, she distances herself from the event, laughing at her outrageous behavior and piling public shame on top of her private guilt. We can trace the chronology of women's aggression through each of these stages.

Holding Back the Anger

As I listened to these women speak, I heard the tension between anger and self-control. Men's anger was uncomplicated by restraint and guilt—it was straightforwardly about winning and losing. But women had cornered the market on the seething, unspoken fury that was always threatening to explode.

Anger was something Cindy had lived with for nearly two years, since the day she met her fiancé's eighteen-year-old daughter. Since her fiancé's divorce, he and his daughter had enjoyed a decade of newfound intimacy and trust, which Cindy's arrival threatened. The daughter, wary of expressing outright hostility to the idea of her father's remarriage, was bent on sabotaging Cindy. She would forget to pass on phone messages, criticize Cindy's clothing and hair, and refer as often as she could to her father's previous relationships with women. Soon after she recognized what was happening, Cindy was driven to distraction by the small but irritating daily conflicts. She didn't discuss them with her fiancé for fear of casting herself in the role of wicked stepmother-to-be. Although no single event amounted to anything significant, the slow accumulation of fury became harder and harder for Cindy to control. The technique she used to control it is a familiar one:

> When I get really angry I think I overreact, and I have a tendency to fly off the handle and say things I really would regret. And I find that if I can give it overnight, by the morning then I'll say what I mean to say and not hit below the belt. What seems to be the difference between men and women is that women will kind of push back and push back on physical aggression until there's no other choice, until things have got to a point where there's no other choice. But men are thinking differently. They're thinking, "If I hit this person, then I'm fighting. I've got to win it, because I'm going to show them that I'm stronger." If we go to hit, it's just because we're *angry*. Frustration. Just rage and frustration.

Cindy's rage erupted one evening at home after the three of them had been out drinking. Although the two women did not actually come to blows, her fiancé was frightened enough to separate them physically and send them both to their rooms. They were, he observed later, absolutely hysterical. Like many men, he was appalled at the sheer depth female anger could reach and decided that he had the right to exercise control over his women.

But the majority of female aggression is directed not at other women but at men, especially those with whom the women live. Stress is more acute in intense and exclusive relationships, and anger, as these women see it and as research confirms, is related to stress.[2] Frustration reaches the boiling point more easily when we have no way to escape the person or the setting that is provoking it. The women in the group talked about domestic battles of every kind, but one of the biggest triggers to their anger was frustration with men who evade, deny, or downright ignore their attempts to resolve conflicts. When a problem arises in a relationship, women's inclination is to talk about it.[3] In childhood, discussion is the female vehicle for conflict resolution, and, by adulthood, it comes to be valued for its own sake as a means of establishing and cementing relationships.

Men, however, tend to treat language as a vehicle for conveying facts and for establishing hierarchy and dominance. From boyhood on, males use language to compete, to outdo, and to top the stories of their peers.[4] It is a means for achieving these ends. There is also a typically masculine reluctance to vocalize internal and intimate feelings. The acknowledgment of emotion comes close in many men's minds to wallowing in self-indulgence. Complex and conflicting emotions like those we all experience in marriage are for most men inaccessible and ineffable. The combination of women's need to share intimate problems and men's need to avoid them leads couples on a circular pursuit in which the woman chases after a conversation that the man does his best to avoid.[5] This denial of the right to express their feelings often throws women into extreme frustration and finally anger.

Caroline was caught in exactly this trap with her husband. A successful trial lawyer, he was renowned for his sharp and incisive performance in court. But at home he sought to avoid any confrontation on domestic matters. He simply would not discuss feelings or emotions—his own or anyone else's. Home was the place he came to for respite. In the end the marriage failed because Caroline simply could not tolerate his refusal to communicate with her:

> It was over an issue that was going to make or break our relationship. And I was so angry because he wouldn't talk to me about it. He gets very close—he reaches a point and then he closes off. A blind drops in front of him and that's it. I'd never encountered that before in my life. I could always wheedle anybody to get a little more out of them, maybe because I was a debater in high school. I could always squeeze a little juice. Not with him. He just used to walk out and that was it. I don't know what's more frustrating—when someone walks out on you in an argument or when they say, "I won't discuss this anymore." I mean it's horrible when someone walks out on you, because you're left with all this frustration, but at least you can scream or kick things or something. But if somebody just turns off because they don't want to talk about it or just sits there, I either have to do something physically violent or leave.

The invisible mental fight between anger and restraint inside the woman is common. Women identify the essence of themselves with the forces of self-control. They are not angry people by nature. The anger, though firmly located inside them, is brought into being by the insensitivity, bullying, or condescension of others.

Like most women, Caroline keeps her anger in check because she fears the awful depth of fury that may drive her to destroy relationships with the people who are most dear to her. "If he saw what was inside me," such women often think, "he would leave." Once upon a time, intelligent women pretended to be stupid so that men would not have to fear them. Although to a great extent women have cast aside that kind of dishonesty, most still cannot own up to their own aggressive impulses. It is men who must be recognized as the masters of aggression and be protected from the knowledge of these same feelings in the opposite sex. A woman who is unafraid to speak out and to stand her ground suggests to many men a woman who sees horizons beyond him. And a woman who, like a man, would sacrifice a relationship for an issue is not the lifelong companion that most men want.

Karen had held her tongue throughout a four-year marriage in which, as a good Catholic girl, she knew her place. Brighter than her husband, she learned to conceal both her intelligence and her anger with the mundane life they led. After her divorce, she moved from a small New England town to New York City, where she became a vice president of a major bank. It took many years before she was willing to marry again, and this time, as she explained, she knew what she was looking for:

> I think that one of the reasons I fell in love with Bob was because I found someone who I was not afraid to have a fight with. That I really felt that I could be horrible—not afraid that he would get disgusted and leave, that my anger would just be too much and that would be the end of it. It became apparent that Bob would take whatever I had to give out. With Bob, you know, he makes me nuts sometimes, and I just go on and on. And he let me know very early on that he was not going to leave me if I got angry, and he wasn't going to argue with me. He wasn't going to get angry with me. That was just how he put it. And he doesn't. But he lets me get hysterical, and then it all blows out. I get my point across and sometimes he says, "Yes, you're right," and it cools off. But it's the security of knowing that I can argue with him.

Like Karen, not only are most women frightened by men's rejection of their angry side, they themselves fear this corner of their consciousness that seems to have grown more vitriolic and more poisonous by its long denial. In the intimacy of marriage, people come to know each other's deepest secrets, and this knowledge can be a terrifying weapon. Perhaps by dint of their greater sensitivity, empathy, or capacity to listen, women often possess a greater armory of intimate knowledge than men. In the heat of anger, might they one day use it against their partners? This fear surfaced often in the discussion that night. Harboring secrets about their partners' insecurities, fears, and indiscretions, the women seemed to say a silent prayer for the victory of self-control and the preservation of souls.

The Price of Victory

Women take a deep breath and choke back their rage—for the time being at least. But often the victory seems Pyrrhic. Doing nothing in the face of perceived injustice may be what women (and some men) expect from themselves, but it can leave a bitter aftertaste. When Karen began working at the bank, she was in a junior position with very little power. She found herself being used as a pawn in the tactical power games of the men around her. Knowing she was being exploited but not daring to risk confrontation, she maintained an appearance of self-control that in the long run won her recognition and promotion. But the daily frustrations exacted a considerable emotional price:

> I was right, and I knew I was right. And I was very junior to this person, and I was real cool on the telephone and I handled it. He was being very nasty. I called and asked him for something and he just lit into me, and it was a result of this long, ongoing argument with my boss. So I was sort of the scapegoat and I knew it. When it was over, I hung up the phone and I cried. I didn't cry because I was upset with myself or I felt like a helpless little female. I cried because I was so angry.

Karen's experience points out an important corollary: By swallowing their anger, women rarely receive public applause. Other people mistake their self-control for indifference or downright acquiescence, and the situation that gave rise to the conflict simply recurs—only to fuel higher levels of anger.

In work situations, all eight women had encountered discrimination, condescension, and harassment. But they all felt unable to fight it. How could they complain, they reasoned, without jeopardizing their jobs, or gaining a reputation for being a trouble-making feminist or for having no sense of humor? What made things even more frustrating was that the men who used these tactics knew that the women were helpless and took advantage of women's self-control. Karen recalled with anger the indignities she had suffered and the anger she had swallowed on the way up:

> You get this frustration because you are risking too many other things to react. Because people are very aware of what they're doing, and they're very aware of the reaction. And you're helpless. Not helpless in the little female sense but helpless in the way that you can't react like you would in a personal situation. You know, I'm sure you've had the same thing, it's when someone's being friendly but you know they're being covertly sexual. And you can't say, "Don't call me 'honey.' Don't ever speak to me again." And you have to see them all the time. *You* know you're caught in a game with them, and *he* knows you're caught in the game. But you can't call the game because to do that would make you seem like a hysterical female.

Caught in the web of others' expectations that she behave like a lady, a woman internalizes these strictures in the form of guilt about expressing aggression. If she erupts she risks public condemnation, but if she restrains herself she feeds the source of her anger with her own frustration at failing to take a stand.

Crying It Out

One route is open to women for releasing frustration without physical injury and without public condemnation. Crying, completely feminine and completely victimless, is the line of least resistance in discharging tension. When Karen became the scapegoat of a male colleague, she had to clamp down on any expression of overt aggression but she did not need to exercise the same degree of censorship over her tears. Men are not threatened by tears as they are by anger because, for them, crying means remorse and contrition, not, as the women know, frustration and rage.

Nora, temporarily away from the demands of the office, found plenty of frustrations in her daily life at home caring for her first baby and working as a free-lance insurance reporter. Mornings were spent playing with her daughter, praying that she would take a nap to coincide with Nora's telephone appointments. If the baby stayed awake, she would have to find a way of keeping her quiet so that she could balance her notebook and telephone and keep her mind clear enough to conduct the interview. Nora lived in constant fear that her professional image and her job would be in danger if an interviewee were to hear her baby crying in the background. Not surprisingly, the stress took its toll, and tears were a frequent result:

> For me anger is so closely bound up with crying. I can't remember getting angry and not crying first of all. I think it's bound up with being kind of helpless. Guilty feelings about actually being angry to begin with. It's very difficult, at least for me, to just scream at somebody and then feel like, clunk, that's over, I got it out of my system. Because I usually break down in tears. I feel so overpowered by the anger, and I really don't know how to express it. I feel like I really don't know how to be appropriately angry, if there is such a thing. Or at least I think there should be a way to be appropriately angry, and I don't seem to be able to do it. So I get very frustrated and then I cry or whatever. Because several times in work situations or if I'm angry at friends or something, I will start out full of righteous indignation and very angry, and it usually comes out in sarcasm—very cool and collected. But then I start to feel myself getting overwhelmed. I know I'm going to break down. And then I get very upset, you know, because I'm going to start crying, and that kind of ruins everything.

Nora's feelings were echoed by the other women in the group. Crying served as a private release but, especially in the workplace, was seen to be thoroughly inappropriate. A woman who is crying is vulnerable; the normal facade of competence has been stripped away.

But weakness also resides in the association between crying and childhood. Tears may underline a woman's femininity but they also highlight her lack of maturity in a world that defines it in the masculine sense of invulnerability.

Cindy had worked as a flight attendant before the pressure of the job became too much for her and she settled down to work in commerce and earn a business degree. She vividly recalled breaking the cardinal rule against crying on the job and the sense of embarrassment she felt with her temporary loss of control:

> It was one of my first flights, and this woman was being such a bitch to me. And she said something to me like I was stupid. I don't remember exactly what she said, but I got so angry I started yelling at her. And I said, "How dare you talk to me like this?" I started crying, and I had to run away. It was so stupid. I got so angry at myself for crying and she caught me crying.

Crying is a problem in intimate relationships for different reasons. When the first flush of romantic tenderness has worn away, men can view women's tears as a tactic or a trick to win an argument. Nora was convinced that her husband thought she cried as a ploy to make him feel guilty and so transform the argument into a sympathy session: "He gets furious. He says 'There you go again—crying because you know it's going to work. You know it's going to make me feel guilty.' " Because crying is judged by men to be childish or, even worse, manipulative, this important channel of tension release is lost to women. Without any means of expression, the stress builds higher.

The Eruption

When the level of frustration becomes intolerable, women are as capable of physical aggression as men are. Karen's story is typical. She is describing the night she knew her marriage was over:

> I dated my husband three years. I married him and I was married four years, so I was seven years with this man—always nice, always easygoing, always absorbing, absorbing. But I was always thinking,

> "If I pick a fight or if I say something wrong, he's going to leave." Because I was very insecure that way. And it was just building up, and so something snapped and all the anger came out. I'll tell you what I did. I can't believe I haven't thought about this in fifteen years. You know it was an argument that was rational. "You're not working and you should be doing this and you should be doing that and you're not doing any work." And all this was coming out, I think, because in my mind I had an escape—the idea of a divorce. And we're talking fifteen years ago and it wasn't respectable. When I finally had that as a rational alternative, I could fight. I could let out the anger. And it was just something that touched me off and he was saying, you know, "You've just got to accept things the way they are. You're looking for a pie in the sky and *this* is what life is," and, you know, he was just trying to brush me off when I felt I was really right. And I flung a teakettle across the room. We had an apartment with one of those folding doors that was plastic. And I ripped it down. I mean this was physical, physical anger. The strength that I didn't know that I had just ripped it down because I was calling attention to the fact that I was so angry. And I left. I just left and that was it. I walked out of the marriage. There was never any thought of reconciliation.

This was an unremarkable act of aggression. No one was hurt. There were no criminal charges. But Karen's account of that moment of violence contains all the elements of women's expressive representation of aggression. It is a story of tension not between her husband and herself (although that was certainly present) but between order and anarchy. On one side are the forces of good, always "absorbing." But what is it that she is mopping up? Not only the anger of her husband but her own rage that she cannot express. Like a good housekeeper, she keeps the mess at bay. She must defuse his anger by listening to his problems and offering support even when the problem is herself. At the same time she must control her anger at the problems she faces, including the problem of being the source as well as the absorber of his anger. She does all this not out of love but out of necessity, to keep him from leaving her.

But her husband has not threatened to go; it is only Karen's insecurity that prompts her to believe that he might. Year after year the tension builds until finally there is a light at the end of the tunnel of her frustration: divorce. If she leaves him, she no longer has to fear that *he* will leave. With that fear gone, she does the unthinkable and starts to complain about the imbalance of work responsibility in their relationship. But her husband doesn't fly into a rage at her. He doesn't threaten to walk out. He isn't a monster at all. Instead he tries to calm her down, in his own way, by reassuring her that all relationships have problems and that she is expecting too much.

Why, then, is her response so extreme? She recasts his reply as condescension, as a refusal to take her seriously, as "trying to brush me off"—because she has already decided that she is going to lose her temper. After seven years she wants to make a mess and let someone else clean it up. Notice that even before she begins complaining, she knows that something has "snapped." Her anger that has been building is only partly directed at him. It is also directed at her own impotence, her own patience, her own control. With control gone, what does she do? First she throws a kettle across the room, then she tears down a plastic door. And what is the point of all this? Clearly not to change her husband's behavior, because she leaves the relationship after the incident. Clearly not to injure or hurt him, because she throws to miss. The point is to "call attention to the fact that I was so angry."

A similar dynamic can be heard in another story of domestic aggression told by Caroline, ten years younger than Karen, an ex-dancer and waitress who is a mother of two:

> We had a really terrible fight. It probably was about nothing important. I can't remember what it was about. But it did terminate with him going in and taking a shower, and I was furious! I just sort of whirled around and I tried to pick up the phone. I don't know if I wanted to throw it, but I knew it wasn't going to go far enough. So I picked up this frying pan that was right there and I tossed it right through the curtain. I didn't even think about it and then he came out dripping, holding the frying pan. And he said, "You could have killed me! You could have killed me, do you know that?" I still didn't realize I could have killed him because I didn't feel like I wanted to kill him. I mean, it wasn't even in my head at the time that I was throwing it. I could have flung it against the wall. I just threw it at him. I really have a very blind kind of rage sometimes when I seem to get really crazy.

When the lid blows off a woman's anger, there is a tremendous fury waiting to boil over. Perhaps that should not be surprising, given the years of slow simmering that have gone before. But women's aggression, unlike men's, is not directly aimed at establishing physical victory—even, as in Caroline's case, when it does. Women explode as a means of release, and it can take the form of anything from throwing pans or kettles to kicking and biting. (Injury as a side effect of, rather than a reason for, women's aggression is explored more fully in chapter 9.) A woman fights to show that self-control has lost the battle with anger. For her, physical aggression is about losing, not winning.

"Look What She Did"

Women are painfully conscious of the fact that their explosions of physical violence are considered bitchy, hysterical, or just plain crazy. Time and again the women I spoke to returned to the issue of the double standard of aggression. Though they thought it right for women to challenge this injustice by expressing their aggression, they usually judged the cost of doing so too high in terms of public disapproval—even in circumstances where a woman had been clearly victimized.

Cindy vividly recalled how she had been pestered by a man in a subway station during her rush-hour trip to work. The train was approaching and he was standing close to her on the crowded platform. Quite suddenly, he deliberately touched her buttocks, and just as suddenly she felt overwhelmed with rage. She spun around and shouted, "Keep your hands off me!" Before she knew what had happened, she had slapped him in the face. The train doors opened and she jumped onto the train, while he remained on the platform. She described the train ride to the next station as the longest five minutes of her life. Everyone in the car was staring at her, possibly in wonder and delight at her response. But as far as Cindy was concerned, the expression on their faces bore a far more sinister message: "They looked at me as if I was a crazy woman." Suzanne had learned the same lesson. She summed up the dangers of expressing aggression: "If women do articulate their anger in some way, they sound like a bitch. Or a hysterical female. And you don't want to fall into that stereotype. And we always have to be little ladies too. It's still a situation where you are told, 'There's frustration and you have to learn to accept that.' "

With friends and lovers, the reaction is a little different. Some men seem to find their women's aggression endearing and funny—provided, of course, that it isn't directed at them. They take it as evidence of the woman's high spirits. Anita was surprised to learn that her husband took an amused pride in her willingness to stand up for herself when Nora told her, "He brags about you. He brags about it all the time. 'Don't mess with her!' It's that kind if paternal 'She's a spirited little gal.' It's cute."

But other men find women's aggression very threatening, feeling that they have sole rights to the territory. Josephine remembers a night when she came close to exploding:

> My husband and I had a fight with this guy over a parking space. I had driven past and then all of a sudden, as we were parking, he comes back and says, "Gee, I was going to take that." Well anyway., we parked and waited for a minute. He came around the block once more, but we were standing there watching the car. Then when we left, we figured that was it. And when we came back, he had bashed in the middle of the car. I'm sure it was him. But when he had come by the first time, I had copied down his license plate. I was all set to find the car and bash his hood in. I would have done it but David said he thought it was inappropriate. He felt it was lowering myself to this guy's level. He frequently lowers himself to other people's level, but when I do it it's like, "Oh, honey, please leave it alone. It's not your business."

Whether met with downright condemnation, a patronizing smile, or a warning to behave properly, women's aggression is always subject to censure. Women are frustrated because their aggressive feelings are misunderstood. They hear themselves shouting, "I've had enough! I can't take any more of this!" But their cry for help and sympathy is mistaken for a war cry. Men hear in aggression, whether by men or women, a challenge. And their reaction is either a counter-challenge or a denial of a woman's right to enter the challenging game. Sometimes, as in David and Josephine's case, this is a direct warning to back off. In Anita's case, her husband's amusement effectively tells her that women are not capable of posing a serious threat. For Cindy, the message is that women who use aggression as a means of control are crazy. When a woman reaches the point of aggression, she is desperate. She wants empathy and concern. She is hoping someone will ask, "What is it that has driven you to this point?" Instead she is told, "Be quiet and get back in line."

"Did I Do That?"

The way other people react has implications for how women feel about their own aggression. As women describe episodes of aggression, there is no feeling of heroism, bravado, or pride apparent in their reports—in striking contrast to the men I discuss in the next chapter—but more a feeling of having breached their proper role. The women I spoke to talked a lot about guilt. Their stories were peppered with comments like, "I felt awful," "I don't know what came over me," and "I behaved like such a bitch."

Their embarrassment was also evident. In our daily lives we all cooperate with one another in a kind of dramatic performance, acting out the roles in which we are cast. But if one of the actors steps momentarily out of character and changes the dialogue, the rest of the cast finds itself adrift. Female aggression is just such a piece of unscripted and unexpected behavior. To gloss over the awkward moment, the other actors tend to express their embarrassment in the form of humor. The cast—and the woman, too, if she is a good sport—trivializes and so defuses the gaffe that has occurred.

Barbara is a lawyer married to a sales executive who thinks the world of her. He constantly buys her presents, takes her out to shows, and orders in expensive food so that she does not have to cook after a day working and caring for two children. On her last birthday, James was late getting home. This was unusual for him, and she began to worry. As the hours ticked by and he did not appear, she became convinced that he had been in a car accident. The children were in bed and she was too frightened even to call the hospitals, so she decided to clean the house to take her mind off her worry. At nearly midnight the door burst open and James appeared, somewhat the worse for wear, carrying a very expensive piece of jewelry for her. He was sure that the gift would buy him out of the expected chiding for his drunken state and his late return. It didn't. Shaking with rage, Barbara picked up the vacuum cleaner and threw it at him. The next day she called him at the office, and his secretary could not resist telling her that the whole office had been laughing about the fact that his wife had thrown a vacuum cleaner at James. Publicly exposed by her husband as a harridan, Barbara had no option but to laugh with them.

Josephine remembered the time she found out that her boyfriend had been involved with one of her friends. Not long after she broke up with him, the morning mail brought an invitation to their wedding. Josephine quietly read it and put it in her purse. That night she went to a restaurant with another friend and her fiancé. Try as she might to concentrate on the evening's conversation, she could not. The invitation was burning a hole in her emotions. She describes what happened next:

> I excused myself and I got up with my glass of wine and went to the ladies' room and smashed it against the wall! I didn't want to embarrass my friend in the restaurant. Glass every place. I felt like a total fool. Then I went around picking up the pieces thinking, "You jerk." Every way you say it, it's like a silly thing to do. It's like almost amusing because it's so silly really.

Nora also recalled making light of her aggression, which at the time had been terrifying. The stress of waiting for her fiancé's divorce drove her to a violent explosion of rage:

> I know that the maddest I ever got with Robert was when we fought a lot about his divorce. And it was mostly because I was so furious at his wife, who was not going to give him a divorce even though she was the one who left him. She was screwing it all up and she was trying to get money out of him and stuff. And I was so angry at her but I couldn't let myself contact her. But I would take out my anger on Robert because I couldn't get to her. So I would have huge fights with him. I started like beating on him with my fists, and so he held

> my hands. So I started kicking at him, and he held my feet. So I started trying to bite him. I was sitting there trying to bite him! I was so furious. I had never been in such a frenzy like that, and he just started laughing—because it must have been so absurd. He called me "Jaws" for weeks!

Robert laughs because Nora is patently ineffective in "beating" him and "winning" the encounter—and to men this is the whole purpose of aggression. He laughs also because he knows women don't know how to fight like men. They do comical things like biting people. What men are laughing at is women's woeful ignorance of the goals and techniques of fighting. The big joke is that they do not fight like men. And because women are good sports, they go along with the laughter. Suzanne recalled becoming furious in an argument with her six-foot-two-inch husband: "I remember hitting Peter on the back with a carton of cigarettes. And he turned around and gave me a knife and said, 'Go on, finish me off.' Then we started laughing."

But the humor glosses over a very real problem. Men own aggression. They do not recognize the legitimacy of any other experience of it but their own. They see not the real desperation of women's outbursts but instead an ineffective attempt at their own brand of instrumental control. If it is a passable imitation, she is spunky; if it is a hopeless failure, she is laughed at. For men, aggression counts only when it causes another person to submit and demonstrates their superiority, as we can clearly hear from the men in the next chapter.

4

Fair Game and Fair Fights: Aggression Among Men

GATHERED in my apartment two weeks after the discussion of women's aggression were husbands, lovers, and male friends of the women whose voices we just heard. Despite the similar backgrounds of the men and women and the emotional closeness of the couples among them, the views they expressed about aggression could well have come from beings on different planets. The men spoke of public aggression as a social event, while the women spoke of the private experience of anger and restraint. Men made much of the stage management of the conflict, while women made more of the emotional component of anger. Men spoke about the morality of the rules that govern fighting, while women were concerned with the morality of aggression itself. Men talked of losing or winning, while for women the very act of aggression signaled a kind of defeat. Aggression for men is what aggression achieves socially: It imposes control over other people, and in doing so creates winners and losers. It publicly affirms the masculine hierarchy.

For men, to be at the mercy of another person, whether physically or symbolically, is to be denied respect;[1] and without respect there can be no self-esteem. Thus men aggress to prove to others (and so to themselves) that they merit respect. But this does not mean that their aggressive acts are devoid of emotion. When their reputation is under attack, men get angry. Their aggression is not a calculated decision to win back their personal integrity; it is an almost automatic and well-practiced response to challenge, and it is accompanied by righteous fury.[2] The anger they feel is at the impertinence of another person's attempt to devalue or humiliate them. Unlike women's anger, it is about redressing social standing, not about catharsis.

Although the situations described by the men in the group as triggering anger and aggression varied greatly, they had in common a perceived threat to the man's sense of personal integrity, his pride, and his mastery of the social environment. Take Peter's story about a familiar situation: wasting a day at home waiting for a workman from a utilities company to install an appliance. This could be an anger-provoking situation for anybody because of the boredom of being forced to stay home and the annoyance at being kept from tasks and activities we would normally be doing. A woman might interpret this situation as frustrating, but Peter transforms the situation into one of power. The issue, for Peter, becomes one of social hierarchy: "You've got to be there from eight to five to get a telephone installed. This guy shows up at three fifty-five in the afternoon, and I'm stuck there. Why, when I'm paying, do I have to be beholden to these people who should be there at our request? We're paying the money. That's what's driving me crazy. We're talking about guys who do this job who can't put two sentences together. Why the hell do we have to put up with this? We're paying them." Peter is not really outraged about the frustration of not having a telephone or the tedium of a wasted day. It is the insult of being made to wait by social inferiors that gets him. It is an inherent slight to his dignity.

This sense of hierarchy and the failure of inferiors to behave with suitable deference is a crucial element in the workplace, but it operates in opposite ways for women and men. While women's anger often erupts from being manipulated or humiliated by their superiors, men's usually arises when inferiors challenge or even question their authority. John, a bartender, felt he had the right to eject troublemakers from his bar. Robert, a reporter, thought he had the sole right to ask questions and dictate the terms of his interviews. In the stories they told, both men resorted to aggression, physical in one case and verbal in the other, to establish who was in charge. Mike, working on Wall Street as a high-ranking newcomer, was vulnerable to the kidding of a less senior but older man who saw him as a yuppie. Mike did not lose an opportunity to correct him on their relative social and material worth:

> I'm in a situation where the major firms will come in and they'll give an order, and they may have weeks to decide whether it's a good buy or a good sell or not. And they'll come in and go, "How are they?" And you give them a market. Then you have literally thirty seconds to make a decision on whether you're going to buy them or sell them, and they have all the time in the world. So you're kind of on the edge. So this one guy comes into the crowd all the time, and he doesn't see the big picture. And he thinks he's very important because he makes his little thirty thousand dollars a year and has his house out in Jersey and eight kids and everything. And he comes in and goes, "How are they? Come on, how are they?" Here's this loser rushing me, you know. And I just said, "Hold your pants on!" He goes, "These rookies. I tell you they really can't make a decision, you know." I really got pissed off because here I am—I mean, I'm trading company money. This guy is like an errand boy. And I said, "Don't give me any shit because you have a know-nothing job and you're going nowhere." And I just kind of let him have it.

Mike pulled rank to let it be known he would not tolerate disrespectful behavior from colleagues in a lower position, but outside the workplace there is much less certainty among men about who is the boss. The right to take charge must be negotiated and even fought over. Any infringement upon the autonomy of another can be seen as an attempt to control and demean. Fights can erupt when one man corrects another's scoring in a card game, accuses another of taking his parking space, or pushes his way into a line of people. A common situation is for one man to decide he is the arbiter and enforcer of "appropriate" behavior and to cast the other in the role of wrongdoer.[3] When one man assumes the mantle of power, the other is left with the choice of either accepting his subordinate status or fighting for the right of self-determination.

In a small New Jersey town, two groups of young men were already on a collision course for conflict, but violence was effectively provoked when one of them decided to correct his enemies' lack of social skills in public: "These kids had come there to start trouble. So we were there eating hot dogs and we were sitting on the hood of my friend's car. There are all these girls around. And one kid starts urinating on the sidewalk. So my friend says, 'Why don't you go behind the bushes and have some respect for the girls?' So the kid said to my friend, 'So who do you think you are? The mayor?' And then they started fighting."

To question a man's behavior or, worse still, as in this case, to criticize it is to assert his intellectual or social inferiority. And, since childhood, men have inhabited a world that is acutely sensitive to issues of hierarchy. They are primed and sensitized to such challenges. Although the logic of this view of power requires that someone accept the role of subordinate, generations of men have refused to believe that it could ever be them. Deborah Tannen perceptively observed the sexual politics of dominance in her analysis of apologies.[4] In saying "sorry" we accept, however briefly, a subordinate role. When a woman receives an apology she frequently returns it with one, as if to release the giver from the temporary state of subordination. When a man receives an apology, he is much more likely simply to accept it, seeing it not as a favor but as his rightful due.

"I'm Not Looking for Trouble"

Among men it is understood that there are those who "look for trouble," actively seeking aggression in order to demonstrate power. For such men, aggression is not reactive—as proper aggression should be—but rather a way to "be somebody." "Real men" should *respond* to challenge with some form of verbal or physical retort, but those who frequently *generate* confrontations are trying too hard to reassure themselves of their autonomy and virility. Jerry, whose laconic style and sarcasm had initiated more than one neighborhood fight, summed up the party line on the subject: "I would never pick a fight. I would never go up to someone and pick a fight ever. But I'll allow people to push me enough for something to start. I'd never pick a fight just for the sake of picking a fight." The real man never looks for trouble, but somehow it always finds him.

There is a clear distinction between being brave and being fearless. Bravery resides in overcoming fear. Most men aspire to bravery. They will fight when they must, despite their natural trepidation about being injured. But men who claim to be fearless, as many fight initiators do, are simply liars. In order to make a legitimate claim for bravery and to distance themselves from a posture of macho swaggering, most men admit to anxiety when a fight is imminent. They make it clear that they are not looking for physical violence but only for a measure of respect. According to them the "ideal" fight is one in which, by dint of sheer will, the challenger simply withdraws before any blows land.[5] But if the opponent steadfastly refuses to show contrition for his offense and to relinquish his assumed control of the situation, then the moment of truth has arrived. The decision to proceed to physical fighting in spite of one's fear is what Mike called the "fine line":

> You don't want to fight the guy. I want that guy to know I'm going to beat him, and I want him to back down. I don't want to hit him. I want *that* guy to be the guy to say, "OK, we're not going to fight." I want to maintain my self-respect. That's the kind of person I am. I just want to get one up on him and then walk away and go "Ha-ha." It doesn't work that way most of the time. This is the problem. You take that one extra step—you can't walk off. It's the fear that's exciting. You're wired. Psyched. You start shaking. Adrenaline is flowing like crazy. Isn't there that one point, though, when you know there's this fine line? You know it. And you're standing there and you realize, "OK, this is the line. I take one step over this, we're going to be all over each other."

The adrenaline-charged decision to step over the line arises from the tension between physical risk and public respect. To back off minimizes risk of physical injury but maximizes loss of face. But the very act of entering the fray, regardless of whether the conflict is won or lost, is sufficient to avoid any imputation of cowardice though it may be physically dangerous. The propelling force for men who seek violence may be the active desire to demonstrate courage, but for most men it is the negatively charged need to avoid being a coward. Another factor is also at work: the audience. To retreat unobserved might hurt a man's self-esteem, but to be seen retreating by others is a different matter. For most men the risk of a black eye or a cut lip is more acceptable than the risk of being labeled a wimp by the community of male observers.

Robert's career as an actor may have attuned him to the importance of audience response. He was honest about the seductions of playing to the gallery:

> There comes a point when I don't know if I do it for me or for acceptance. I think maybe you first start doing it for yourself and you really get pissed off and you get in there and start something. And then you realize that people are listening. And it's kind of uplifting because you're on stage, you know. Everyone is going, "Ooh, look at that over there!" You feel good. You kind of feel like, "I have some power here. I have something over them."

But crossing the line in search of personal integrity happens only in particular situations that have passed the test of fight-worthiness. Male aggression occurs in the public sphere and is subject to public rules. Victory must be come by honestly; private and public acclaim for fighting rests on certain moral conditions being met.

On any given occasion of conflict, a man faces three discernibly different scenarios in terms of risk of injury. The first is when the odds so favor a victory that to use physical force could only be construed as bullying. The second is when the odds so favor the opponent that victory is only a remote possibility. In the third, the fair fight, the opponents are evenly matched. Each of these scenarios has its own dynamics, logic, and social consequences.

Fighting with Good Odds: The Bully

Robert remembered one night when he was eighteen coming home visibly drunk. There was an argument with his father, who made a move to hit him. Robert pushed him aside and felt a blinding urge to punch him. He knew for the first time that he was facing his father as a man and that it marked the end of his childhood. With equal clarity, he realized that the man he was looking at was old. He restrained himself not just because it was his father but because of the obvious differences in their physical strength and agility.

Women are included in this "no-go" category regardless of their strength or fitness. The men I spoke to were vehement and unanimous about their abhorrence of physical aggression against women. As well as being a prohibition handed down through the generations, its rationale is not lost on men. They know that the obvious differences in physical strength between men and women make any kind of contest dangerously uneven. As Jerry put it:

> I never have hit a woman. I mean I would never do it. I've wanted to. Many times. But we have physical strength over them and that's just not fair. It's the old male thing. Let's face it, if you are accused of woman beating, you're a marked man. If you're living in a lower-middle-class area where people live a really hard, tough life, if you punch out your wife and you go back in that local bar and your wife comes in with a shiner, you are a marked man.

The notion of frustration, salient in women's accounts of their aggression, rarely surfaced in these men's stories. The exception was when they discussed their wives. Peter, married for twenty years, still struggled to live up to the moral imperative against hitting women. He succeeded by simply leaving the scene of arguments while he was still able to control his temper: "The frustration level hits the point where either you say, 'You ignorant bitch how could you be so stupid?' or you take a swing at her or you do something else. Then what I usually do is go to the bar. Or just get the hell out of there." The only situations where men, like women, must restrain their desire to lash out are when the contest is so uneven that aggression could only be seen as bullying. And it is here that men's words seem to echo those of women. But while women's self-control results from their view of aggression as an unacceptable behavior, men's self-control is called upon when the other person is an unacceptable target. Women's restraint is based upon generalized *values,* while men's is based upon specific *rules* of conduct.

But if men oppose the idea of aggression against women, how can we explain wife beaters? Perhaps they are men who do not subscribe to the rules of conduct which outlaw it. The facts suggest otherwise; both men and women abhor wife beating,[6] and even men who beat their wives say that they do not approve of their own actions.[7] They join in the denunciation of violence against women because they know that a man's aggression, when it breaks the rules of fight etiquette by picking on a weaker target, never wins applause. They cannot command respect and gain self-esteem by boasting about beating up a woman. Though many men use violence to control their wives in private they do not brag about it in public. Instead they recite the accepted rule of male aggression, that bullying is not fair fighting.

Fighting Against Bad Odds: Heroism and Youth

In the opposite situation, when the odds are severely stacked against him, a man faces a real dilemma. Fortunately for him, whatever choice he makes, the social consequences will be positive. He can withdraw, because the rules of fair fighting have been broken and he is released from any honorable obligation to fight it out. Or he can enter the fray; so much the braver. Going forward against the "bad guys," whose refusal to play by the rules clearly identifies them as bullies, confers a particular heroism upon him.

Of all the factors that constitute a bad-odds scenario, the most common is sheer numbers. When the man (and his friends) are grossly outnumbered, the possibility of victory is low and the likelihood of injury high. Facing such an episode, John decided that a tactical withdrawal was the best way out:

> I went outside the party with Owen and we were hanging out, waiting for them. Because there were only three or four of them. All right—Owen is huge. I was cocky at that time. I was pissed off because these guys were genuine jerks. They had this ego thing. Plus they weren't smaller than we were. So I felt justified if we got into a fight. I was just mad. They struck a nerve. I don't know what it was. So we went outside and we waited for them to come out. We were leaning on the car waiting for them to come out. They came out and then we realized that there was a carload of them out there. So words were exchanged and we got in the car and left.

Territorial concerns are also important. Fighting outside one's own territory is an inherently bad-odds situation. The very fact of being an intruder on other men's turf is a provocative act to which locals are likely to respond with hostility. Also, the intruder does not know the social ropes and is more likely to commit a local cultural gaffe that might lead to trouble. Finally, being out of one's own neighborhood ensures that there will be no friends to be counted on and no knowledge of the terrain, which might be needed for a fast escape.

Peter recalled an incident during a visit to England. One Sunday morning he had set out on foot to explore London and soon found himself in a rough part of town. He noticed a pub, which, although rundown and uninviting, had its doors open. He walked inside to find a menacing group of young men propped against the bar. Peter was lost and had to get directions to the nearest subway. His American accent triggered a string of hostile remarks. Insulted and angry, he was well aware of being out of his own territory. His only option was to get out of there fast. But several years later, the failure to face down those young toughs still left a sour taste: "I just sort of pulled back, walked and left. I wish I could get those kids."

Another bad-odds situation is a confrontation with the "crazies," who inhabit so many cities: criminals, drug addicts, ambient psychotics, and potentially violent homeless people and teenagers. Not bound by the social conventions that lend order to daily life, crazies are unpredictable. They are free to jump people from behind, throw them on subway tracks, verbally or physically assault children or women, and employ a variety of orthodox and unorthodox weapons. Robert was once on the subway in New York when a crazy was intimidating a car of riders:

> We were in a train and it was crowded and we were going along, and there was this one guy who was really disheveled and everything but obviously drunk—and there was a nun on the train. This guy is driving her crazy, talking to her and being very vulgar. You know you can feel a crowd moving? There was no way this nun was going to be hurt, it was all verbal. If this guy made a move in any way, shape, or form, this guy was going to be taken care of. But in the meantime, no one was going to make a move to start something with this guy. The train pulls into Wall Street. All of a sudden this one guy who was obviously a construction worker of some kind got up, took the guy by the neck, literally lifted him up, and threw him out, and the entire train cheered.

In spite of Robert's protestation that the offender would be "taken care of," there was considerable reluctance by all concerned to start a fight until they were in the relative safety of the station. Bad-odds situations present a clear choice between fighting and fleeing. In conversation at least, there is a marked preference to dwell upon the first choice. To enter the fray in spite of overoverwhelming odds is the zenith of male courage. But in retelling bad-odds stories, whether the outcome is a win or a loss is of little moment. A man's mere engagement in battle assures his listeners that he has "balls." Such stories are apocryphal tales, a few good men facing the wrath of an army of villains. Or, in Jerry's case, an army of college students:

> My favorite story is me and four friends. Anyway we were all in this university town full of students. Anyway, we're all drunk. It's ten-thirty. All the bars shut at ten-thirty. So we go to this party. We're basically getting into having a good time, drinking beer, and for some reason the guy who's throwing the party decides he doesn't want us there. Bad mistake. There's only five of us, about fifty of them. One of my friends was drinking a pint of cider and this guy took it out of his hand and said, "We don't want you here anymore." So Chris took it back and just poured it over this little bastard's head. So therefore we're standing around expecting this guy to hit Chris and thinking what will happen then—because Chris will kill him. And of course, he doesn't hit him. His wife comes up and hits Chris, pushes him. And Chris is a gentleman. He doesn't do anything. He just lets her punch and punch. And she does eventually knock him over, because he's a big lad. When he falls over, ten of these little bastards come round and start kicking him. Michael realizes what's going on, picks up a bottle, and goes *crack!* on about three of their heads. The bottle never breaks—that's the first mistake of all films. Then I see someone grabbing my wife's hair and banging her head. So all hell breaks loose. A massive, fantastically wonderful fight ensues. Great feeling when you're with all your friends. Five against fifty and we won.

Jerry and his friends enthusiastically joined the fight, but what of bad-odds situations in which men choose not to engage in violence? In a male culture that equates submission with effeminacy, how is it possible for them to admit that they walked away? They cope with this dilemma by shifting the link between aggression and manhood into a new rhetorical gear: aggression and youth. Fighting becomes the prerogative of the young and foolhardy; retreating the benchmark of maturity.

The men who spoke that night were able to shift from one to the other of these modes of interpretation with ease, as long as the case for maturity was made only for bad-odds situations. The trick to telling such stories is to highlight the realism and maturity of the decision, playing down any element of fear. Dwelling on fear in a bad-odds situation tends to suggest that the retreat was driven by terror rather than mature judgment. John remembered an incident from his youth. At the local mall he and a friend saw two tough-looking kids, one of whom was wearing a furry hat. John and his friend pointed at the hat, barely able to contain their amusement. The two strangers approached them and threatened John with a gun. His response bore no imprint of the fear he must have felt at that moment. Using the incident as a way of demonstrating his coolness and maturity, he said to them, "Look, if you're going to shoot me, go ahead. If not, leave." When one of them told John to leave instead, they argued a little. Then the strangers left. That's when, John explained, he learned that "if you can argue your way out of it, it's better."

Peter, the oldest of those at my apartment that evening, seconded the wisdom of withdrawing, adding some fatherly advice: "I've found that as I've gotten older, I've learned how to get out of fights more than getting in them. When I was a kid I would just throw punches and regret it later. But now that I'm older it's a question of maintaining your own self-respect, being tough and yet knowing how to talk your way out of a situation."

Picking on Someone Your Own Size: The Fair Fight

In fair fight or equal-odds situations the two men are evenly matched and here the man has no choice but to go forward with the fight. Even situations that begin as fair fights can be altered by any move that breaks the rules and so confers an unfair advantage. The men spoke of being jumped from behind by their opponent's friends after the initial engagement and of opponents who suddenly and unexpectedly produced a gun. But if the rules of propriety were honored, such fights are retold with a feeling of enjoyment, satisfaction, even humor. The fight can be a harmless expression of high spirits or a means of cementing camaraderie. Most men feel no sense of guilt or remorse afterward. After all, in such fighting the gentlemanly code is upheld and no serious injuries are sustained. It is not much more than an adult extension of the routine physical encounters of boyhood. For a few minutes, all eyes are on the fighters, as courage is established and reputations are made.

Robert remembered a night when he left his local bar with his wife and several friends. Spilling out onto the sidewalk, they were saying goodnight and preparing to head their separate ways home. Two men walked by and, without apparent reason or provocation, one of them insulted Robert's wife. By the time he had digested what had been said, the men were halfway down the block. Robert sprinted after them and demanded an apology from the one who had called his wife a "dog." When he did not apologize, Robert delivered a hefty punch to his face. The tussle continued, watched by an audience of observers whose role was to ensure that the fight was conducted properly. It wound down when Robert upended his opponent into an open garbage can. His friends, satisfied that Robert's honor (and that of his wife) had been restored, obligingly seized him from behind and assured him that the offender had had enough. Robert allowed himself to be led away from the scene, protesting, but not too vociferously, that he had not finished with him yet.

This is a classic fair fight: an insult is thrown; the insulter refuses to comply with a demand for an apology; the way is clear for physical engagement to determine whether good or evil will triumph. But it is hard to avoid concluding that the best moment of any fight is its retelling to an appreciative audience of men. The danger over and the fear a rapidly dimming memory, all that remains is the glorious moment of excitement and the sense of masculine camaraderie. John remembered his youthful fights with typical affection: "To me it was an enjoyment, a joke. My friend would start it, and I'd get into a brawl with him and maybe two other guys. Then after the whole thing was over, we'd have a drink together and laugh about it." Whatever men do in terms of aggression, there is a rhetorical presentation that can justify, glorify, or celebrate it. It is a no-lose situation, in contrast to the no-win situation it is for women.

If social representations not only explain past events in a particular way but actually drive our behavior, then expressive and instrumental representations should be able to explain the unique patterns of aggressive behavior the two sexes display. The shape of male and female aggression has been carefully documented by social scientists over the last forty years, but to date it has not been satisfactorily explained. It is to this task I now turn.

5

Gender and the Shape of Aggression

A WOMAN sews peacefully while her husband rampages up and down the room cursing at her. Two friends sit together over a cup of coffee complaining about their husbands. A woman shakes with rage, crying and screaming uncontrollably. A wife calmly cooks dinner while pouring rat poison into the stew. Images like these have spawned a folklore about women's aggression, which claims that women are placid and just don't feel anger the way men do, or that women are "bitchy," "hysterical," or "catty." Are these images pure fiction or do they, in common with many stereotypes, contain a grain of truth?

As we have seen, men and women speak differently about the meaning of aggression. They rely on these views not only to interpret past events but to guide their behavior. People who believe that aggression is a loss of control will express anger in a different manner from those who believe it to be a way of exerting control. If we are right about the ways in which men and women differ in their understanding of aggression, we should be able to make sense of their differing behavior. In moving from social talk to social action, we also move into the realm of research studies that have drawn unique profiles of men's and women's aggression based on hundreds of subjects in laboratory and questionnaire studies.[1] Men's and women's representations of aggression allow us to formulate predictions about the particular patterns of action that should result from them.

Anger

Becky is a happily married woman most of the time. But between six and seven o'clock in the evening, things go wrong. Her husband, irritable after a day at the office and an exhausting commute, pours himself a drink and settles down to watch the evening news. A glass of wine in hand, she joins him after a day in which she has weathered her daughter's tantrum in the supermarket and a major run-in with her son about the state of his bedroom. The television brings its usual torrent of bad news—diplomatic failures, murders, tax increases, job losses—and her husband begins his usual tirade about the ineffectual government, the impotent criminal justice system, and the general moral decline of the world. He rants his way through the broadcast while she sits quietly. Suddenly he turns to her and exclaims: "Don't you care about this stuff? Doesn't it make you mad?" No matter how much she protests, he doesn't believe she is disgusted with the state of the world. If she were really angry, she would show it. It is a short step to his familiar accusation that she is a vegetating, apolitical housewife, and once again they are launched into a fight.

The tendency to become angry, even enraged, by events can be seen as an aspect of personality. Certainly people differ in their responsiveness to the aggravating business of daily life, but do women and men as groups have different personalities? Can we say that women simply do not experience anger as deeply or as often as men?

A personality approach assumes that within each of us is a given amount of a trait—hostility, for example—and that this trait expresses itself in our reactions to situations.[2] People who have very hostile personalities would then be expected to show more aggression in their dealings with other people—regardless of when or where they encounter them—than those with low hostility. But such an argument neglects a critical factor that operates between personality and action: thought. And this is where social representations are located. The critical difference between men and women is not in their personalities but in their thinking, and their differing beliefs about what their hostility or anger means is manifested in their actions.

Of course, there are individual differences within each sex too. Some women are far more willing than others to express anger, but this stems from differences in the degree of stress they are under and the level of self-control they are able to impose. Some of us have to let off steam all the time, while others may need to only once a year. Likewise, aggressive men tend to be those who have been successful at using aggression as a means of controlling others or of maintaining their self-esteem. Men who lack the basic physical strength to manage violent encounters are unlikely to seek them out, as are men who are able to establish their self-esteem in other areas of their lives. Women's ability to control their reaction to anger should not be misread as implying that they do not feel it. To do so would, among other things, do a great disservice to the restraint that women impose upon themselves.

Paper-and-pencil questionnaires such as the Buss-Durkee Hostility Inventory have been used to search for gender differences with regard to anger. With questions such as, "I don't let a lot of unimportant things irritate me," and, "Sometimes people bother me just by being around," these tests are designed to tap aggressive feelings, covert hostility, and hostility turned inward. But no sex differences have been found.[3]

Another way investigators have examined the issue is by asking men and women to keep a diary or to recall specific experiences of anger. A survey of a wide range of men's and women's emotions shows virtually no difference in the frequency with which they experience anger—or fear, joy, or sadness, for that matter.[4] Over a period of one week men typically get angry between six and seven times, women between five and six times—a difference so slight that it could not possibly account for the magnitude of sex differences in aggression that we see all around us.

But if men experience anger more strongly, even if no more often, then this might provide a useful clue to differences in aggression. Again, the sexes do not differ in the intensity of anger that they report.[5] However, one study found a sex difference in the relation between the intensity of anger and its duration. For men the two are only slightly connected; for women, the more furious they are, the longer it takes them to get over it. (Another tantalizing finding was that women not only rate their anger as equally intense as men's, but they also believe that their anger is out of proportion to the events that cause it. Once again, women's greater guilt creeps in where men's does not.[6]) The authors suggest that "when a woman becomes intensely angry, she tends to inhibit expression of her anger, thus prolonging the episode"[7]—and, as with some of the women we heard in chapter 3, becoming even more enraged at her own passivity and impotence.

If women get angry as frequently as men, yet lash out far less often, then anger and aggression cannot be directly connected. In fact, in some instances they are quite irrelevant to each other. Boxers, wrestlers, army recruits, and criminals all use physical aggression without feeling angry. One group of researchers contrasted laboratory experiments in which subjects were made angry with similar studies in which no anger was raised; men, far more than women, proved capable of acting aggressively even when they had no personal grudge against their victims.[8]

Once again, the point of men's instrumental aggression is not to signal emotional upset or to let off steam but to control the behavior of another person, and this can be done as effectively, if not more effectively, when anger does not get in the way. Men's strategic use of aggression as a means of instilling fear and gaining power is vividly captured in this statement by a self-described relentless bully in the workplace:

> You could almost smell the fear, and that made me feel powerful. No one could get the better of me. . . . I can honestly say that not a day went by when I didn't shout at someone. I used to tell them if they wanted to keep their jobs they'd have to do things my way. No one else's methods were as good as mine. If I asked someone into my office to discuss absences, I'd stare at them for a while before I spoke. Then I'd accuse them of not being able to handle the job, tell them that if they kept taking time off they obviously couldn't cope.[9]

Such cold and calculated aggression finds its most sinister expressions in the exclusively male crime of rape and the predominantly male crime of robbery, both of which nearly always demand an aggressor who feels no anger toward the target of his violence. What is coercion for some men is cruelty for women because anger is a necessary component of their aggression. For men, it is sometimes an optional extra.

From Words to Blows and Tears

Words, as well as blows, can be a very effective means of hurting other people. Psychologists have confirmed that women's language use is superior to that of men.* But the stereotype translates women's fluency into the idea that they specialize in bitchiness and verbal aggressiveness, while men's penchant for physical aggression is often seen as being up-front and direct. (Yet, old adages notwithstanding, most of us would rather suffer a torrent of abusive names than spend the evening in the emergency room with a fractured jaw.)

Surprisingly, men outdo women in terms of verbal as well as physical hostility.[11] And considering a typical incidence of aggression makes the reason clear. A husband comes home from work one evening and opens the conversation by observing that his dinner is late. When his wife tells him to give her a break, he reminds her that he works harder and makes more money than she does. She tells him to cook the damn dinner himself. He curses and swears. She calls him an animal. He throws a plate at the wall.

Detailed studies of criminal violence confirm that, by the time people come to blows, they have already engaged in a battle of words.[12] There is a fairly consistent sequence underlying most assaults: there is a disagreement; person A demands that B retract, make amends, or leave the scene; B refuses to comply; A threatens; B counterthreatens; third parties intervene to calm things down or heat things up; finally, A hits B. The same sequence of escalation from verbal to physical aggression has been demonstrated in studies of domestic violence. The more disagreements a couple had, the more verbally aggressive they were. And the more verbally aggressive they

*Indeed, women's superior language skills have prompted theories suggesting that brain lateralization is more symmetrical in females, allowing for greater transfer of information from the nonlinguistic left hemisphere into the language-using right hemisphere. In men, it is suggested, the left hemisphere operates more independently, denying access to the other half of the brain and possibly making it more difficult for men to verbalize essentially nonverbal experiences and abilities.[10]

were, the more likely they were to be physically violent toward one another. There were virtually no cases where a couple fought physically but did not argue.[13]

But men move from verbal to physical aggression much more readily than do women. Women need a greater push before reaching the point of violence—and that push clearly relates to their level of stress at the time. In a national survey, the violence rate of wives was half that of their husbands when the women's level of stress was low (as measured by the number of recent stress-producing events, such as having a baby, moving, or experiencing sexual problems). But at the highest stress level, the rate of assault by wives was 150 percent *higher* than that of their husbands.[14] As we would expect from women's expressive view of aggression, their violence may be a long time coming but its potential is there all along.[15]

When women reach the breaking point and act on their anger, it looks very different from men's. Marital violence studies show that the most prevalent form of violence by husbands is "pushing, grabbing and shoving," but wives tend to lash out blindly to release their pent-up rage and thus show far less control and direction. They not only push, grab, and shove but they also throw things, slap, kick, bite, or hit.[16] This behavior appears to men to be truly senseless, because it does not achieve the "obvious" instrumental goal of dominating another person. But women's thoughts at such moments are likely to be along the lines of, "Get away from me. Leave me alone. I cannot stand to be on the same planet as you right now."

In chapter 3 I discussed how the biggest single sex difference in response to feelings of anger is that women cry. It may be their greatest resource when it comes to discharging tension without causing injury. Interestingly, the tears that we shed when we are in the grip of extreme emotion are chemically different from what we produce when we are slicing an onion; emotional tears contain stress chemicals that are manufactured by the body when we are cornered.[17] When suddenly overtaken by a state of panic or distress, we can use up stress chemicals by taking dramatic action such as attacking an opponent or running away. But when we are conflicted or immobilized, our body cannot discharge them in the same way, so they find their way out of the system through tears. Women, well trained in the suppression of their own aggression, often find themselves in this kind of conflicted situation, and a "good cry" settles down the tension, the racing pulse, and the pounding heart without hurting anyone else.

Men tend to take a dimmer view of women's crying. In a popular self-help book about marital fighting, the author describes women's crying as just another fight *tactic.*[18] But at the point of tears, a woman is well beyond gamesmanship. The psychologist Robert Averill is one of the few researchers who has explored the meaning of women's tears. According to his study, 78 percent of women who cry during fights do so out of frustration. If crying were a successful "tactic," it would bring an argument to a close. Yet in 80 percent of cases where women cried during a fight, they did so at the beginning or middle rather than at the end, and 55 percent of women who cried did not begin until *after* the fight, when they were alone or with someone other than their antagonist. For many women the distress lingers on until they can discharge it in tears.[19]

The Who and Where of Gender Differences

Suzanne was working as a cocktail waitress while she finished her master's degree. A few years earlier her parents' marriage had nearly collapsed because of her father's affair with another woman. Suzanne's mother had tried to kill herself. One night Suzanne saw the woman sitting at a table in her bar. Carrying a tray full of drinks, she passed the woman's table and spilled six cocktails onto her. When Suzanne told us this story, there was laughter as well as astonishment. This story was utterly unlike the other women's experiences of aggression, not because they had never thrown anything at anybody but because they had never done it in public and certainly never at another woman.

We would expect women to become aggressive with men rather than other women and to do it in private. As we have seen, the taboo on aggression between females is a lesson learned in childhood.[20] "She went last time, so it's your turn now" or "Let's play something different if everyone is going to get angry" are the kinds of solutions that girls develop in the face of conflict that threatens relationships.[21] This works well as long as everyone values people over issues, but not if a renegade in the group righteously sticks to her position to the point of violence. International diplomacy also worked fairly well until terrorists started breaking the basic understanding about how business was to be conducted. In the world of couples, men take on a role similar to the terrorists'. They seem determined to escalate issues as a point of honor, seeing them as more important than the relationship itself.

At first, women react with a mixture of embarrassment and amazement to their partners' determination, for example, to argue a point on a Trivial Pursuit question and to their raised voices at dinner parties. Men, as women see it, just don't know when to let it go. Later women may find that their willingness to concede a point in a domestic argument is exploited rather than appreciated, and that their low-key tactics don't stand a chance against men's brute force. And this is why women are far more likely to explode at men rather than at other women.

A woman is also more likely to erupt in aggression in private than in public because her anger is likely to have been piqued by her partner at home. Also, she is acutely sensitive to social condemnation and considers aggression self-indulgent and shameful. Audience approval is the last thing she is looking for.

Men's instrumental view of aggression leads to different expectations. Men should be most aggressive to other men in public and least aggressive to women in public. The seeds of men's antagonism toward their own sex are sown in the structure of their childhood groups.[22] Because their relationships are established in a more public sphere (unlike the clandestine secrets whispered between girls), the pecking order is available for everyone to see. Rough-and-tumble play, contact sports, and especially aggression are the commodities that are traded to climb to the top of the heap. All of this cut-and-thrust is constrained by the basic rules of fair fighting. Kudos can only be gained by beating someone else "fair and square"—by confronting them openly and by being *seen* to do this by as many boys as possible. When boys become men, they must modify their willingness to physically fight. But the rules live on, even in the more sedate encounters of the dinner party or a game of "Trivial Pursuit." Dominance means a head-on public confrontation until someone climbs down or, failing that, until someone (usually a woman) intervenes, pleads for restraint, and allows both parties to back off without losing face.

Certainly men do not want to be seen behaving aggressively toward women, but that does not mean to say that they are unwilling to use it when no one is looking (see, for example, chapter 6). Years of boyhood training are not easily cast off in marriage. When under threat—and with regard to women that threat is almost always to their superior status rather than a physical challenge—many men assert themselves as loudly and ferociously as they can. They may not be at the top of the male hierarchy but they are certainly not going to be dominated by a mere "woman." If verbal attacks fail, some men will escalate to blows, but rarely in public.

The data bear out these predictions. *Both* sexes are indeed more likely to behave aggressively toward men than toward women.[23] Don Fitz and his colleagues asked people to recall four angry episodes: one in which they said nothing, one in which they discussed their annoyance with the opponent, one in which they screamed at their opponent, and one in which they had been physically aggressive. Women were less likely to be on the receiving end of all four kinds of anger, but especially so for physical aggression. The tendency for men and women to express their anger against men is particularly marked with acquaintances and strangers. Outside of intimate relationships, over 80 percent of aggressive actions by both sexes were directed at men.[24]

Women's aggressiveness toward men has been difficult for social scientists to explain, believing as they do that women avoid aggression in general because they are afraid of retaliation and injury.[25] But if this is true, why do women more often fight men rather than other women, even though men are far more dangerous opponents? Nowhere is this more apparent than in extreme cases of criminal violence by women. Women who commit murder are more likely to kill members of the opposite sex than are men. If we are right that women aggress only when they have reached the breaking point, then fear of retaliation or physical danger should not be an important consideration. In extreme states of emotional arousal, women are not thinking about the consequences of their actions.

Fitz found, as we would expect, that the tendency for men to choose other men as their opponents is particularly evident in public situations, but not one woman in his study reported public aggression against a member of her own sex. Wherever the aggression occurred, men's aggression, both verbal and physical, had twice as many onlookers as women's. The most extreme difference was in physical aggression outside the home, where men's aggression drew an average audience of nearly six, while women averaged less than one onlooker. Although some instances of women's aggression may be strictly defined as public (occurring on a street or in the lobby of a bar, for example), this does not necessarily mean that anybody is there to see it. In fact, there was no difference in the number of spectators between women's public aggression and their aggression in the home.[26] When a woman sees someone flirting with her husband at a party, she may control her anger until they both have to use the bathroom or collect their coats and then confront the woman, but a jealous husband will probably take on the issue then and there. And the more onlookers, the more likely he will be to express his anger both verbally and physically. As we would expect, a male audience is particularly effective in encouraging male aggression.[27] But same-sex spectators have the opposite effect on a woman; they seem to remind her of the norms about restraint shared by the community of women.[28]

Guilt and Empathy

Researchers agree that women experience more guilt and anxiety about aggression than men do.[29] In the presence of an audience, an additional element of discomfort is added: shame, which makes her outburst all the harder to live down. Some writers stress the policing role of society's expectations of feminine behavior and, by extension, the relevance of shame.[30] I suggest instead that women's guilt arises from the failure of internal policing. Nonetheless, shame can augment guilt (which is why women more often give way to aggression in private rather than in public).

A number of studies on anxiety and aggression show that women defend against the perception of aggressive content in pictures of interpersonal situations.[31] This same trend has appeared in studies showing that women take significantly longer to recognize aggressive material[32] and distort and delay recalling violent material. People who report the most anxiety about the use of aggression also report that they rarely behave aggressively, and this is especially true for women.[33] In other studies, researchers have interviewed men and women after they have acted aggressively in laboratory situations.[34] Women report higher levels of anxiety than do men at such times, especially when the target is a woman and when the aggression is physical rather than verbal. Some women feel so much guilt that they actually punish themselves for behaving aggressively. In one study, women were divided into three groups. One was induced to give electric shocks to a female partner, another was made to watch the woman being shocked, and a third group sat in a waiting room. Then all the women were offered the choice of giving shocks to a new partner or receiving the shocks themselves. The first two groups chose to suffer themselves rather than inflict pain on someone else.[35]

The first group probably experienced full-blown guilt, but the second group had only witnessed the suffering. This points us squarely in the direction of empathy as a potential cause of the guilt most women feel about aggression.[36] The more we empathize with a victim, the greater the guilt we will feel about our aggression. Do women have a greater capacity for empathy then men? Certainly there is a disproportionate number of women in jobs requiring the care and tending of other people (nurses, social workers, teachers, and so on), which suggests that empathic roles are more congenial to women than to men.[37] And standard tests of masculinity and femininity that reliably differentiate between men and women contain items measuring sensitivity to others' feelings.[38] So women's reluctance to aggress may be tied to a greater ability to respond emotionally to the distress of another person. Clinicians believe that this quality is central in controlling aggression, and a number of successful therapies are explicitly based upon training people to place themselves in the position of their adversary.[39]

Failure of empathy has been held to be crucial in one clinical syndrome that seems to be a peculiarly male diagnosis: antisocial personality or, as it used to be called, psychopathy.[40] Men with antisocial personality seem unable to feel or even comprehend the pain they cause others. This inability stands at the heart of the variety of other symptoms of the disorder—failure to establish and maintain long-term relationships, callous exploitation of other people for their own ends, and a seeming disregard for the consequences of their own actions.

Hans Toch, in his pioneering study of violent criminals, catches exactly the flavor of the antisocial personality:

> This man has a habit of placing other people into the most awkward situations without appearing to realize what he is doing—without anticipating the obvious reactions to his tactless opening move. He isn't aware, for example, that when you cohabit with a woman you just can't come in one evening and simply announce your imminent departure, and then expect to spend a congenial evening with her. Now when the other person reacts—the person who is going to be abandoned or who has just been insulted—then we have a second stage in which our friend sees himself as attacked out of the clear blue sky. He can then be quite brutal while viewing it all blandly as an act of self defense. . . . So he has this pattern of provoking people in a rather selfish way, not seeing the consequences. There is a complete blindness to the other person's point of view.[41]

One psychotherapist has noted that the chief cause of adjustment problems among male clients is an inability to relate to others.[42] Seeing intimate relationships as a weakness and a source of vulnerability, they become pathologically isolated. Women, on the other hand, find their way to the psychiatrist's couch for the opposite reason. They empathize so strongly with others that their own sense of independence is weak. In extreme cases they feel devoid of their own personality. They have become so merged with their mother or husband that they feel they do not exist when they are alone. It is this that keeps women trapped in hopeless relationships. There is clearly such a thing as too much empathy.

When we ask people how they feel when they are on the receiving end of someone's anger, women typically say that their feelings are hurt, while men react with defiance, refusing to acknowledge the legitimacy of the other person's grievance.[43] Because women can acknowledge their own pain when they are a victim of other people's anger, they can attribute it through empathy to the targets of their own anger. Perhaps this is why women believe that their own aggression is more harmful and socially damaging than do men.[44] And if men cannot or will not acknowledge their own pain when they are attacked, then they will certainly refuse to acknowledge it in others. The antisocial or psychopathic male may be only the extreme, deviant manifestation of men's tendency to "close down" emotionally during conflict.

Attitudes: Masculine and Feminine

In a man's world, aggression has a place as the ultimate answer to opponents who refuse to see the truth and fairness of a man's position, provided that it is the *last resort* in a process of power assertion where politeness and decency have failed. The vast majority of men do not seek situations of conflict any more than women do. Nevertheless there are circumstances where men's failure to aggress is taken as simply cowardly or weak.* Women's expressive view suggests that they would see aggression in a less acceptable light and would reserve their worst condemnation for the most clearly instrumental uses of violence.

Opinion pollsters have compared men's and women's attitudes on a variety of contemporary issues and found the greatest difference in what they say about the use of force or violence.[45] In questions ranging from international war to fistfights, men favored aggression more than women on 87 percent of the issues, but there was considerable variation in the size of the gender gap.[46]

First let us consider those areas where it is widest. Many more men than women approve of boxing; many more men describe themselves as "hawks" in their attitude toward international war; many more men believe that "wars are necessary to settle differences"; and many more men support the death penalty. All these issues are essentially ritualized or institutionalized forms of violence. There is no anger in boxing, war, or executions: These are emotionally cold actions in which force is used according to prescribed rules to establish a winner, to take control of a country, or to achieve justice. Men

*The U.S. military used to ask conscientious objectors, "Wouldn't you use force against someone who was raping your mother?" Any reasonable man, the theory went, would have to answer yes to such a question and, by doing so, reveal that he was not wholly committed to pacifism.

also hold more favorable attitudes toward gun ownership and television violence, and they are less likely than women to believe that media violence causes crime.

These issues seem to reflect men's greater tolerance for aggression in society. Indeed, 50 percent of men surveyed, compared with 15 percent of women, own a handgun, and most men oppose any attempts at gun control. As long as the bad guys have guns, the good guys must have them too. Anyway, they argue, if guns are taken away, people would find other ways of killing one another. Even though many of them are fathers, men as a whole are much less concerned than women about the violent fare that is served up to their children on television. It is not that men are uncaring or insensitive. They seem simply to believe that aggression is so intrinsic to human nature—at least to men's nature—that the mere refusal to televise it or to allow gun ownership will have no appreciable effect. Boys will be boys, with or without television and handguns.

Polls that tap aggression at the level of individuals, rather than in broader social issues, show a much narrower gap between men and women. This makes sense, since an act of physical violence between two people can be interpreted as either expressive or instrumental: It might be driven by a sudden loss of control or by a realization that violence works. Consider some questions from a poll aimed at finding out whether people believe the taking of human life is ever justifiable. The first question asks whether executing a person for committing murder can be justified. This question clearly taps the respondent's view of instrumental violence; execution is one of the most rational and institutionalized forms of lethal violence. As we would expect, the gender gap here was large, with more men than women answering yes. But the sexes showed a difference of only 4 percentage points on the justifiability of a civilian taking a life in an act of self-defense, which can be seen as either expressive (a crime of passion resulting from overwhelming rage) or instrumental (a tussle for survival in which the would-be victim seizes control of a lethal situation). The same effect is found for less serious retaliatory aggression: the justifiability of a man punching a stranger in the face. Both sexes answered very similarly for a number of scenarios that share expressive as well as instrumental interpretations, agreeing on the justifiability of counteraggression when the victim had been beating up a woman, when the victim had struck a child, or when the victim had broken into someone's house.[47]

When asked if they would approve of a teenage boy punching another boy, men and women agreed that it would be acceptable if the aggressor had been ridiculed or struck by the other boy. Women probably think such provocation led to an understandable loss of self-control, while men would tend to think of this as a typical adolescent fight for status. But the sexes disagree when the story is changed so that the other boy had challenged the aggressor to a fight; issuing a challenge transposes the situation from one of anger to one of ritualized confrontation, and women do not approve of it.[48]

Queen Victoria, it is said, refused to endorse a law against female homosexuality in England. It was, she insisted, ludicrous to suppose that such a thing could ever occur. Much the same point of view applies to female aggression: Not one of the questions in the poll asked about it. But, as we would expect, men came out more in support of instrumental uses of aggression than did women. To keep all this in optimistic perspective, note that 63 percent of men and 70 percent of women in a national sample maintain that physical aggression is never justified. For the majority of both sexes, aggression is clearly a line of last resort.[49]

The Gender Pattern

There is no shortage of plausible explanations for men's heightened aggression. Biologists argue that testosterone, the male androgen, is the key. Some psychologists blame it on the ways parents transmit to children a double standard about the acceptability of aggression. Other theorists pinpoint male and female adult roles: the tendency for men's participation in competitive sports, the military, and the cutthroat world of business actually to encourage the use of aggression, while women's traditional roles as homemakers or as lower-status employees systematically deter the expression of aggression. These theories may explain why women are less aggressive than men, but they generally fall short of telling us why, when men and women aggress, their behavior looks so different. Why, for example, don't men cry? Why, when women do lash out, do they usually pick on men rather than other women? Why do men hit women in private but deny it in public?

Social representations can offer explanations, and they flow coherently from the simple idea of expressive and instrumental theories. But this does not mean that other explanations are necessarily wrong. It may well turn out that genetic and hormonal factors are important in explaining men's aggression. It may also be that evolutionary biology is implicated: Perhaps far back in our collective history, men's heightened aggression made them better candidates for becoming hunters and, much later, businessmen, politicians, and army recruits.

The roles we live out each day are connected with the way we think about aggression. It may also be that parents perpetuate these roles in the messages they send to their children. A social representation of explanation can make more specific predictions not because it is a better theory but because it is framed at a level much closer to actual behavior. It is a *proximal* rather than a *distal* explanation, which means that it is concerned with factors that are relevant *at the moment* when the action takes place. Distal explanations look farther back in time to find the causes of aggression. Evolutionary biology is just about as far back as humans can see. The effect of testosterone on the organization of the brain is pretty far back in terms of the life of an individual, and so is the way a person's parents reacted when he kicked his little brother as a child. Even our social roles, such as nurse or businessman, are distant and irrelevant to what is in our heads at the time we get into a fight. But the meaning people attribute to other people's actions and their own is important at the very moment when they bite their lip or swing the first punch.

Social representations act as a kind of cognitive glue that holds together one's past history with the future that stretches ahead. They create consistency between our interpretation of past fights and our behavior in new ones. They also glue together society's expectations ("Women don't fight") and our expectations of ourselves ("Fighting is destructive and selfish"). Perhaps they even glue together the demands of biology (low androgens, low aggression) and the illusion of free will ("I choose to restrain myself").

But we cannot forget that social representations are situated in a particular historical and cultural moment. Instrumental and expressive views of aggression make sense to people *now*, at the end of the second millennium in Western society. They organize and explain our aggression as we know it. But there are plenty of other ways to comprehend aggression: possession by evil spirits, temporary madness, suicidal impulse turned outward. These explanations come and go as the form of our knowledge changes and as culture transmits new ideas and concepts around the world. It comes down to this. Women cry rather than hit not because of their hormones, their reinforcement history, or their role as carers but because they see aggression as a personal failure; and the safest release for their anger, when they deny themselves blows, is tears. Men hit not because their testosterone makes them, or because their mothers didn't punish them enough, or because they are account executives but because when they are publicly humiliated by another male, they believe that aggression will restore the status quo. Social representations must mesh with our biology, biography, and social roles, but they are not *determined* by them.

But if the theory of social representations is worth anything, it must be able to address the phenomenon of authentic violence as well as experimental studies and rating scales. In the chapters that follow, three important areas of contemporary concern will be explored to show that social representations can be useful in making sense of the complicated and often frightening world of violence: robbery, violence within marriage, and street gangs.

6

Robbery

MOST of us have a kind of radar for the sound of footsteps behind us on a dark, empty street. But this is not enough to protect us from the crime of robbery. One woman recalled for me her nightmare experience of victimization:

> It was 7 o'clock at night, I was coming into my building. And this big guy all of a sudden came up behind me. He was black and I didn't want to offend him by slamming the door in his face so I let him in figuring "He's probably just visiting a friend—no need to be nervous." The minute the elevator door opened I went in to the elevator and I turned around and he had the door jammed open and he had a knife. He told me to take off my jewellery, put everything in the grocery bag I had and then he hit me—not that hard—but he knocked me down and then he told me to press six and if I told the police he would find me and kill me.

Robbery is the most frequent stranger-to-stranger violent crime in the United States.[1] One in three victims is injured, and one in four injuries is serious. Of all violent crimes, with the exception of rape, robbery shows the greatest imbalance between the sexes. There are between ten and fifteen robberies committed by men for every one by a woman, according to official statistics in the United States, Australia, and Europe.[2] Less than 1 percent of arrests of women in the United States are for robbery.

Robbery is a characteristically male crime. It is alien to women in both its cold-bloodedness and its monetary goal. Robbers have no personal grudge against their victims and feel neither fury nor loss of control.[3] Victims are usually strangers chosen from a pool of candidates who happen to be in the wrong place at the wrong time. The choice, as we shall see, is in terms of how "easy" they look—how successfully it appears they can be intimidated into parting with their money. The willingness to inflict injury for a purely monetary goal also alienates women from robbery. Psychologists, even in the sterile confines of the laboratory, know that money is ineffective in inducing aggression among women. As one researcher put it: "Money proved to have only a negligible effect on the aggressive behavior of females, a finding that seems in accord with the demonstration that money is altogether less salient for females than it is for males."[4] Money is intimately bound up with men's self-esteem. The psychologist Arnold Buss, surely thinking only of men, proposed three major incentives for aggression: money, status, and prestige.[5] Sadly, in the case of Western men, these are far from independent categories. In the workplace, success is reflected in the unholy triad of wages, seniority, and power. The measure of a man is the thickness of his wallet, and it is the surplus cash—over and above what is spent on immediate material needs—that is the real index of a man's status. Men are not more materialistic than women, but for them wealth brings prestige. And nowhere more so than among men denied by unemployment the opportunity for status through work.

In addition to the monetary payoff of robbery, there is the thrill of the encounter—a competition of bravado in which one of the participants must lose. When Bernhard Goetz turned the tables on half a dozen would-be robbers in a New York City subway by pulling out an illegal handgun and firing, the public support that swept after him seemed to transform this gaunt, bespectacled young man into a cult hero. Many robbers privately admit to the thrill of seeing naked fear on their victims' faces—a far cry from the terrain of women's aggression. Robbery is perhaps the purest form of instrumental aggression. So quintessentially male is this crime that its gendered nature has been overlooked. Few people have posed the question, Why don't women rob? But before I can state that it is because of their social representation of aggression, I must first consider more concrete solutions to the question.

Tough Enough

One explanation for the gender difference in robbery is the fact that males, on average, are larger and stronger than females, and robbery often involves physical confrontation. Robbers work hard at maintaining their strength and speed. One study found that 72 percent of robbers were concerned with keeping fit, and 54 percent had received some fight training in the military, at martial arts centers, or as professional boxers.[6] The developmental path toward robbery lies along urban streets, where young men stage mock fights as a form of entertainment.[7] In a game called "yoking," for example, one boy runs up behind another, locks his arms around the unsuspecting "victim's" neck, and effectively incapacitates him.

This and other street games encourage youths to perfect the physical skills necessary for mugging, the forerunner of true robbery. Mugging is junior league in two important respects: It relies wholly on speed and agility (very much a young man's game), and it does not require that moment of face-to-face confrontation with the victim that constitutes both the thrill of robbery and the demonstration of the robber's courage. Boys graduate to robbery when they acquire the cold confidence for the facedown, in which they must bet that the threat of violence alone will give them victory.

But as persuasive as the physical strength argument seems to be in accounting for the gender gap in robbery, there are problems with it. First, the smaller size and lesser strength of the average woman is a handicap *only* if she selects men as her victims. A same-sex robbery is no more physically dangerous for a woman than it is for a man. But in the small group of female robbers, the choice of victim closely matches that of male offenders. About 53 percent of women's robbery victims are men, and the remainder are evenly split between women and mixed-sex groups.[8] This strongly suggests that it is not concern about their physical weakness that holds women back from robbery.

Furthermore, if women's lesser strength were at the heart of the gender gap, there would be a similar imbalance in other violent crimes. Yet the sex ratio for assault is far less skewed in males' favor: Men outnumber women here by only about 3 to 1.[9] More dramatically, the rates of cross-sex domestic homicide show a ratio of around

2 to 1. Among married and dating couples, violence is used equally by both sexes,[10] as we shall see in the next chapter. Women, given sufficient provocation and stress, are quite willing to assault men—even men who are twice their size. What is foreign to most women is the instrumental and cold-blooded exercise of aggression as a means of coercion.

In any case, women have the option of equalizing the encounter with a gun. Faced with an armed robber, only about 25 percent of victims offer any resistance. (And wisely so. Victims are about twice as likely to avoid being attacked during an armed robbery when they comply.)* And women do not seem especially handicapped in obtaining or using guns. In homicide an identical proportion of men and women—46 percent—uses handguns to kill their victims.

Do female robbers use guns to eliminate strength disparities? Studies of imprisoned women suggest that they do: Three-quarters of incarcerated female robbers in a 1988 study had used guns.[12] But—and it is a big *but*—these figures are based on the most serious robbery cases, where the women received a prison sentence. A national survey of crime victims tells us about a wider spectrum of robberies, including those never reported to the police. Here we find that only about 30 percent of female robbers (compared with 50 percent of males) used a weapon.[13]

Diminutive size and strength are apparently not a worry to women who rob. And, indeed, statistics suggest that women's confidence is well placed. Although far fewer women than men use weapons, they are no less successful in their crimes. Measures of theft completion (incidents in which offenders secured the money or valuables they demanded) show women's score, at 64 percent, to be 2 percent *higher* than men's.[14]

*Over the last few years there has been an increase in the use of handguns in robbery, particularly in the United States. Between 1979 and 1987, 639,000 violent crimes were committed with handguns in the United States, a third of them robberies (equaling 18 percent of all robberies). When handguns are present, fewer crime victims sustain nonfatal injuries (only 15 percent) than in robberies when handguns are not involved (31 percent). Victims of handgun robbery, however, are much more likely to lose property and ten times more likely to be killed. Indeed, robbery is the most frequent stranger-to-stranger crime that results in death and injury. Victims of gun-toting robbers are twice as likely to die as those robbed by an offender with a knife.[11]

Money, Risk, Thrill—and Posturing

Most robbers say that money is their primary motive.[15] The majority of them are either unemployed or in casual jobs, and most have tried other forms of criminal activity but found robbery the most convenient. It requires little skill or equipment and offers immediate hard cash. As one man put it: "It's the fastest and most direct way to get money. There's no thrill in getting it. It's for the cash, the money, that I do it. . . . One armed robbery pays about as much as 20 burglaries."[16]

But if money is the motive, we should all be watching our backs when a woman follows us down the street. In the United States there are 150 women for every 100 men living below the poverty line.[17] The feminization of poverty has been the result of the enormous alterations in traditional family structure. About one-quarter of children in the United States are living with their mothers only, many below the poverty line. For single mothers, child-support payments are often nonexistent or sporadic, so they must rely on their own employment or welfare to pay the bills. Yet the jobs that are available to them are low-paying and offer little possibility of escape from poverty. Lack of child-care facilities keeps many women out of the labor market altogether. Given the desperation of many women's lives, it is remarkable that so few turn to robbery. Susan Jones is one who did—and became the subject of a sensational newspaper headline:

> MOTHER TURNED TO CRIME TO PAY DEBTS
>
> Susan Jones took on day, evening and night jobs after her husband was made redundant [laid off], the court was told. But after losing one of the part-time jobs, the "devoted" mother of twins, who housed her father, a sister and an aged aunt, was diagnosed suicidal and then turned to crime. Philip King, council for the defence, said: "She led a double life, a robber by day and a devoted wife and mother by noon, evening and night."[18]

Instead some turn to nonconfrontational means of making illegal money. The criminologists Darrell Steffensmeier and Michael Cobb examined sex differences in crime rates from the mid-1930s to

1980. Robbery showed no significant change over the forty-five-year span. But the sex differential for petty property crimes (larceny, shoplifting, forgery, and fraud) rose steadily over those years, accounting by 1980 for almost 40 percent of female arrests. As the authors concluded:

> These offenses do not require masculine attributes such as the use of force or confrontation with the victim but fit well into the daily activities of women, such as shopping and paying family bills. Furthermore, the skills required for forging credit cards, writing bad checks and shoplifting are learned in the normal process of growing up. Those arrested tend to be amateurs.[19]

These are women who cannot pay their utilities bills or the food they have ordered in restaurants. Women who run neighborhood numbers games to make a few extra dollars or who lie on their welfare applications. Women who stuff food inside their coats because they cannot pay for it at the supermarket checkout counter. We should be grateful that women are "amateurs" and that they don't possess such masculine "attributes" as the willingness to threaten and injure.

The financial motive that spurs men's robbery is not born out of desperation. Only 18 percent of robbers say they need the money to support themselves or their families. For the rest, it is used to finance drug use, to buy alcohol, and to pay gambling debts. Seventy-nine percent of robbers spend the proceeds solely on clothes, cars, and vacations.[20]

The criminologist Jack Katz believes that thrill is an important part of robbery and that its appeal is exclusive to men.[21] When the veteran robber John Allen went straight, he recalled: "I like to stick-up. I like the risk. What I really missed was the excitement of stickup."[22] The risk is the possibility of losing the robbery confrontation, and the confrontation is about power. When the offender demands that the victim "hand it over" or "give it up," he is referring not only to money but to control. If the victim laughs, pulls a gun, or kicks him in the stomach, then control has been seized from him and with it his tough image and self-esteem.

Many robbers speak of the adrenaline rush that goes with the standoff: the heart races; the hands sweat; breathing rate increases;

and muscles tighten. They are in what psychologists call a state of nervous arousal, the building block of emotions. Experimental studies have demonstrated that this excitement can be labeled differently depending on the individual's interpretation of the situation.[23] Thrill and fear are not physiologically distinct. The nervous system undergoes the same changes for both. When the body, sensing danger, prepares itself for vigorous action, some men find it pleasant (and call it thrill) and others do not (and call it fear). Either way, it is an acknowledgment that the moment of truth has arrived. He must either seize control or lose it.

But to understand the alleged delight robbers feel in risk, we must be clear about the differences between what they say and what they do. Risk implies that robbers see themselves as facing a situation in which the odds are stacked against them. Yet victimization surveys suggest that this is far from the case. Over half of all robberies are committed by a team of offenders; half involve the use of a weapon against an unarmed victim; two out of three robberies is of a woman, a child under fifteen, or someone over fifty.[24] The possibility of losing the confrontation is minimized by superior numbers, strength, and firepower, together with the crucial element of surprise. The robber knows that the crime is about to take place, but the victim is caught wholly unprepared and must adjust to the situation in a matter of seconds. Most victims are totally confused by the suddenness of the event[25] and, since the average robbery takes less than a minute, the realistic odds of success are heavily on the offender's side.

Robbers are bullies—this is the best instrumental recipe for getting their hands on the money. They may pride themselves on being tough guys, but this image does not fit their exploitation of weak and vulnerable targets such as women, drunks, and children. This is why, in their social talk, robbers create the impression that they face a risky situation and consequently that they have heroically triumphed against superior odds.

This crucial distinction between the stark facts of the event and its dramatic retelling has been all but lost on many researchers. It is not simply a question of robbers fooling the interviewer; it is a question of fooling themselves.[26] Robbers seem to prefer to dwell upon their confrontations with able-bodied men. The sociologist

Robert Lejeune's account of robbery comes very close to capturing their contradictory worlds of talk and action:

> Respondents, for example, have predispositions for or against mugging women (generally against): for or against mugging old people (generally against): for or against mugging whites rather than blacks (generally for): and for mugging the rich rather than the poor (always the rich). These predispositions, if implemented, would tend to limit mugging victims mostly to relatively young and affluent white males. In practice such predispositions are not unimportant but they appear to play only a secondary role in the selection process when compared to the more vital concerns of reducing personal risks and of locating a victim within the usually limited temporal and spatial scope of the stroll. Thus, for example, while the predisposition to mug men rather than women is verbalized by most respondents, this preference is easily eroded in the attempt to select the most accessible or vulnerable target.[27]

Lejeune is one of the few who sense this misleading quality in robbers' accounts. Usually they are taken at face value, so that we can wind up all but admiring their compassion: "We don't rob those poorer than ourselves, it doesn't make sense. It's a form of job for us, it's a form of valor. To rob working people is not right; maybe these people make no more than $200 a week."[28] (In fact, the victims of around 60 percent of robberies earn a total family income of under $15,000 a year.[29]) Contrast such noble sentiments with this description of a real-life robbery:

> Two males estimated to be between 25 and 30 confront a man and wife who are out for a mid-afternoon walk in their neighborhood. One displays a knife and demands money. As she fumbles to hand over the $3 she then possesses, the offenders notice that she has gold-filled dentures. Before fleeing, they forcibly extract her bridgework, remove her diamond wedding band, and take $6 from her husband.[30]

Only about one-third of robbers engage in the macho rhetoric of thrill and risk.[31] The majority view it more expediently: Their focus is single-mindedly on the money, and violence is their tactic for obtaining it. These men are in the business of robbery not as a crutch to self-esteem but as a form of work, and so they are more straightforward about the tactical desirability of minimizing risk and maximizing reward. As one of them put it, "I was looking for somebody looked scared to me when I looked at them. You know, people give off vibes. You feel this guy looks scared. He'll give it to you in a minute."[32]

Furthermore, the belief that female criminals avoid risky crimes is simply wrong. Prostitution is often held up as the female alternative to robbery,[33] and it is a crime involving considerable danger. Many prostitutes are brutalized by both customers and pimps as a routine part of their lives.[34] Each time they enter a car or a hotel room with a stranger who may be twice their weight and strength, the odds are stacked against them in terms of violence. The argument that a different attitude to risk is behind the gender imbalance in robbery seems less plausible than the more obvious point that a robber uses instrumental violence to coerce and exploit. If prostitution is quintessentially feminine, it is in the mutuality of the exchange and not in the relative riskiness of crime.

Men's Streets

About 70 percent of the robberies in the United States, Europe, and Australia are spontaneous. But the opportunity for a spur-of-the-moment robbery can arise only when a robber is where the action is. And the action is on the streets, where four out of ten robberies occur. In poor urban areas, thoroughfares have achieved a significance far beyond mere architecture. To grow up "on the streets," to be "streetwise," and to have "street smarts" all carry a particular meaning.

But ethnographers who write about street-corner men rarely mention their female counterparts.[35] The streets are about masculinity and danger. Many ghetto men, particularly those with no domestic base, spend a good proportion of their waking hours on the streets. But even married men may congregate on the street to wile away the unemployed hours and to get out from under their wives' feet. Women who pass by are tolerated or ignored, or else they become the butt of playful (or not so playful) sexist remarks. They are guests in a male environment, always outsiders to the real business of the male club. Pimps, strong-arm studs, numbers runners, winos, and hustlers meet, talk, and go about their business in a nonstop forum of rapping and male bonding, with its characteristic tension between mutual support and mutual competition. One powerful means of testing and solidifying group cohesion is the joint commission of crimes. As Lejeune has noted:

> Mugging, particularly at first, is most often a group activity. It occurs with the urging and support of peers or under the guidance of more experienced associates. Under such conditions of high observability the outward manifestation of fear is likely to be curbed and the expression of bravado is encouraged. The group pressure which evokes this bravado represents an active force toward the collective minimization of the perceived risks associated with take offs [muggings] and other predatory acts. By reducing the awareness of danger the situation becomes normalized. Even the most narrow escapes and profitless endeavors are transformed through group interaction into humorous, daring and worthy enterprises.[36]

This atmosphere is supported by heavy drinking. Over 70 percent of opportunistic robbers admit to having been drunk at the time of the offense. As psychologists have discovered:

> The perceptual distortion that accompanies drinking and dampens the drinker's awareness of the environment also reduces his view of the complexity of the world. In other words, the situation to the drinker may appear much simpler than it is otherwise. This, in turn, enhances his sense of control and may contribute to the *feelings of mastery and power some men exhibit* when under the influence of substantial amounts of alcohol.[37] [Emphasis added.]

The male environment, the feeling of power, and the apparent simplicity of the world can come together in a potentially dangerous way in the hatching of robbery. Peer pressure to go along with an ill-conceived rip-off is high when men are drinking together, especially when the friendships are intense and emotions volatile. At the same time, the drinkers' primary aim may simply be to continue drinking together even when legitimate funds have been used up. In such a context, the consequences of a robbery may seem remote indeed.

Could it be that the absence of women from urban streets is the explanation of women's distance from robbery? Victimization data tell us that a third of robbery victims are women. If women are in such locations as victims, why aren't they more represented among the offenders? Perhaps they are excluded from the male groups in which robberies are planned and executed, but there is nothing to prevent them from planning robberies in the privacy of one another's homes. Yet the proportion of planned to unplanned robberies for the few women who do rob is the same as that of men.[38] It is not the mere absence of opportunity, for opportunities can be created where there is a desire. Women do not cajole one another into acts of instrumental violence by accusing each other of being "chicken." In general, they do not see their aggression as a means of exploitation or control. Is there something, then, about the act of robbery that makes it difficult for a woman to pull off?

Threat and Bluff

Robbery is composed of four stages: (1) the offender establishes co-presence with the victim; (2) the offender announces the robbery and gains the victim's compliance; (3) there is a transfer of material goods; and (4) the offender leaves the setting.[39] In the first stage, the robber will often exploit the stranger's kindness in order to gain proximity. He may ask for the time, a light for his cigarette, or change for the phone. The female robber has a clear advantage at this stage—a fact that the convicted robber John Allen notes in his autobiography: "Of course, broads always got the advantage, especially when it comes to sticking up drug dealers. A dude will let a broad in his home any time, cause he's not expecting no dangerous move from her."[40]

The key to executing stage two is to create terror in the victim.[41] He or she must be made to believe that the robber *will* use violence—indeed, is someone who frequently resorts to cold-blooded violence—if the threat is to be effective. Here the fact that women are seen as less threatening than men works against them. Even though they may be willing to use violence, they are unlikely to be perceived as potentially violent by victims.

But despite the tactical advantages of threatening the victim with a weapon, only a minority of women use one. Because a high proportion of female robberies (like male ones) are unplanned, it may simply be that women do not carry guns with them as routinely as men do. (One study of male repeat offenders found that almost three-quarters carried a handgun most or all of the time.[42]) Or perhaps women robbers balk at the use of deadly force. Either way, because women who rob are weaker and usually unarmed, they attack their victims more often than men do. They are more likely than men to inflict minor injuries such as bruises, cuts, black eyes, and scratches.[43]

There is a logic to this. Offenders with guns harm their victims less often because most victims faced with a lethal weapon decide that discretion is the better part of valor. As one robber vividly pointed out, "You know, if somebody came up to me and said 'Give me your money' and he had a gun or a machete, I'd give him everything. I mean, it would scare the hell out of me. It would scare the hell out of anybody."[44] Women attack their victims as a display of preemptive force or in response to the victim's failure to take the robbery seriously or to comply with the demands. Physical attack has to take the place of menace for women robbers, if they are to reverse, on the spot, the public belief that women do not have the stomach for violence. Once women manage to convince skeptical victims to comply with their demands, they complete robberies with equal "success" as men.

Becoming a "Hardman"

To understand fully the masculine appeal of robbery, it is necessary to refocus attention from the act to the actor and from the moment of the offense to the life-style of instrumental violence of which it is a part. Katz succinctly expressed the attraction of robbery: "Unless it is given sense as a way of elaborating, perhaps celebrating, distinctively *male* forms of action and ways of being . . . stickup has almost no appeal at all."[45]

Men who rob tend to do so again and again: 44 percent of men arrested for robbery are rearrested for the same offense within three years.[46] And this may be the tip of the iceberg, since it counts only official police arrests. For example, one offender who began robbing at the age of thirteen estimated having done over a thousand stickups by the age of twenty-six, yet he had been arrested only five times and convicted only once.[47] But robbers are not specialists; they engage in a whole variety of serious offenses. One study gathered life histories of over two thousand prison inmates in California and found one group of "violent predators" to have been high-rate robbers, assaulters, *and* drug dealers; their involvement in crime had begun before the age of sixteen.[48] Another study spanned ten states and found that the typical criminal was involved in sex, drugs, and guns before he was even eligible to drive.[49]

These men's life-style revolves around the development of a peculiarly masculine social identity. A core concern for them is money—not, as we have noted, to raise their children or to pay the rent but to spend as lavishly and conspicuously as possible. Robbery and other forms of hustling provide it, but the take disappears fast. As one man put it: "I go through it in three or four days. I buy clothes, I go out, I get high. I get shoes, or a knit, or slacks—I get a lot of things I don't need. You just live while the money's there: that's the rule of the street. . . . When I've got money, I don't sleep for three or four days—you're just *buying* something all the time."[50]

Such sprees form part of a binge that often follows a robbery. The purchase of cocaine, crack, speed, marijuana, and liquor fuels several days of committed hedonism. Sometimes a motel room is rented; sometimes the action takes place in a friend's apartment. Friends and acquaintances appear out of thin air to join in the fun and tap into the free drugs. Women may be hired for their sexual services, but more often they provide them gratis in return for a few rocks of crack. Card games run until exhaustion or bankruptcy sets in. Delivery boys appear every few hours with food. And so it goes until the money runs out.

Surplus cash and its lavish disbursement provide rewards over and above the immediate sensual thrills that money can buy. Sixty-eight percent of offenders are under the age of twenty.[51] These ghetto youths are surrounded by the street-corner men who populate their neighborhood stoops, drinking their days away. In their faces, young men see the future that awaits them. Against this backdrop, those who can flash ostentatious style and easy money shine brightly. Not yet worn down by arrests and prison terms, they are, for a few short years, the arrogant energy of the ghetto. Their largess both impresses and indebts others, who are no longer mere admirers but friends and beneficiaries.

But the sprees set up a cycle of "earning and burning" money that takes on a life of its own, as robbers quickly discover: "Since we were spending money so fast we had to pull jobs at least once a week. We'd spend two hundred dollars a day buying everything we wanted. You spend money like this because in the back of your mind you know you can always get more by pulling another job. When we bought wine we'd get six or seven half gallons for the winos and get drunk with them on the street corner."[52] These men become "cafeteria criminals," turning from one hustle to the next as the opportunities present themselves. John Allen reviews his versatile criminal skills this way:

> This is all I know. I know how to steal. I know how to be hard on broads. I know how to stick somebody up better than anything. I know how to take a small amount of narcotics and eventually work it way up and make me some money. Fencing property or credit cards, I know how to do all of that. . . . For a man, pimping is a good way of making money, but the fastest way is narcotics and the safest and best way of all is numbers.[53]

Exploitation is the common denominator of these crimes. The aim is the same: to "get over on someone" and "spot the chumps." Whether it is housebreaking, robbery, roughing up prostitutes, cutting cocaine with cleaning powder, or talking people out of their spare change or life savings, at the end of the day it is about outsmarting others. And robbers are extremely sensitive to the possibility of having the tables turned on them, as Allen explains:

> You know when people are going to rip you off. You know when somebody is up to something. They give their self away, the way they look or the way they act or the way they talk. The amount of money don't make no difference: you just can't let people get out on

> you. It don't matter who you are or what you are; they'll try and you gotta stop them. *At all times you gotta stop them.*[54] [Emphasis added.]

This pervasive sense of competition, of the immanent exploitation of vulnerability, of the dangers of ever letting down one's guard, have a uniquely masculine flavor. Allen's sentiments transcend the lines of social class; with suitable rephrasing, the same ideas might well be expressed by a white-collar account executive. But it is much harder to imagine such sentiments being expressed by a woman. The constant vigilance against threats from other men has a tense, tight quality that betrays a deep skepticism about such "feminine" attributes as trust or dependence. To be exploited is to invite contempt, not sympathy. To rip off is to demonstrate superiority, not brutality. Robbers are masters of callous and casual exploitation, as we can hear in another of Allen's accounts:

> The main thing is getting what you're going after and getting away. Occasionally somebody say, "I ain't giving up nothing." But you can change his tune easy. You ain't got to kill him. Smack him with the gun or shoot him in the foot or kneecap; he give it right up. Knock his big toe off with one of them .45's, he give it up. I think it's probably my background that it don't bother me.[55]

Dissociating himself from his actions and refusing to contemplate that he is inflicting real harm are the hallmarks of the true "hardman" or "badass." It is a state of mind that must be worked on and perfected. On their first outings, most robbers are fearful both for themselves and for their victims. The situation constantly threatens to escape their control, to degenerate into a fiasco or a brawl. In declaring the crime, the robber declares himself to be in charge, and insubordination by the victim is a direct challenge to that control. He feels himself bound to see it through to the bitter end, even when that involves violence. With practice, such violence begins to feel normal. From his initial fear that he may have to make good on the threat, he comes to see violence as a routine aspect of the robbery. As one seasoned robber summarized: "You have to be cold. You gotta show your heart. You gotta show you're not scared to shoot—kill this person if he gives you any hassle. . . . You have to look cool, like shooting you ain't no big deal."[56]

The hardman image finds its zenith in the gratuitous use of violence. A victim who *resists* an armed offender risks an 86 percent chance of being injured or killed.[57] This is a horrifying statistic but at least it is comprehensible: The robber who has committed himself to the crime refuses to give up even when the payoff could not possibly be worth the harm he must inflict or the prison sentence to which it might lead. But the more chilling fact is that *two-thirds of the victims injured in robberies do not resist in any way.*[58] And the most lethal and most frequent use of gratuitous violence is in black-on-black robberies.[59] More than half the victims of black robbers are white, so why should offenders reserve the most senseless and extreme violence for members of their own race? At least part of the answer may lie in the nurturing of their local reputation as hardmen. In selecting local targets and performing on their own turf, they bring into play two important factors.

First, the situation is often a homicide or an assault that turns into a robbery rather than the reverse. The victim may be an ex-associate who informed or withheld proceeds from a joint crime. He may be a "crooked" drug dealer or a rival in a romantic dispute. The theft can be the gratuitous part of a "hit" that would have taken place anyway to enhance the offender's reputation as a hardman who should not be crossed. Second, the hardman's ambition may be well served, since acquaintances and neighbors are likely to hear of the events, making him a highly desirable crime partner.

Women aggress and they steal but they rarely do both at the same time. The equation of money with control and social status requires a masculine logic. For women, as we shall see in the next chapter, violence is the explosive product of pressure and passion in the often claustrophobic atmosphere of the home.

7

Intimate Rage: Violence in Marriage

IT has taken a long time for the public to become aware of violence between spouses. Although the police have always known about it, arrests were rare because the private relationship between a man and his wife was considered off-limits to official intervention. Apart from the firsthand experience of police officers called to the scene, there used to be no reliable information on the frequency or the severity of marital violence. Then, in 1980, the shocking results of the first national survey of violence in the home were published. They showed that a person stood a greater chance of being the victim of violence in the home than on the street. Twenty-eight percent of couples reported physical aggression at some point in their relationship, 16 percent in the previous year alone. Even more remarkable, women and men admitted to almost the same number of acts of aggression toward their partners.[1]

Nor was this confined to trivial acts. Considering only acts of severe violence, 3.8 percent of women and 4.6 percent of men had been the victims of punching, kicking, hitting with an object, or assaults with a knife or a gun. This equality between the sexes in the use of violence against partners applies to cohabiting and dating couples also. Because of the disparity in height and weight between the sexes, women's injuries tend to be far more severe than men's, and the problem of spousal violence has rightly become an issue about the suffering of women rather than men. But of all the forms of criminal violence, it is only those committed in the privacy of the home that do not show the usual marked gender differences. What is it about cohabitation that can lead to this increase in women's aggression? How can we explain the fact that women, so infrequently represented among muggers and robbers, recoil far less often from assaulting the men with whom they live?

The paths that lead to aggression by men and women are very different, even though the raw count of blows exchanged may be the same. In the traditional household, the man returns from the stresses of the rat race to enjoy the ministrations of his wife. Whether employed beyond the home or not, she generally feeds him, cleans for him, launders his clothes, raises their children, and gives him emotional support. These services are an index both of her love and of his worth. Although in the workplace or in the peer group a man must earn power, in the home it is often his right. If he feels his authority threatened in this last bastion of self-esteem, the results can be terrifying. For most women, the roles of wife and mother remain central. Success in the world of paid work may bring pride, but not if its cost is failure at home. And it is in the home, as we shall see, that the delicate balance between women's self-control and level of stress is most likely to be upset.

But perhaps more explosive than either of these two forces alone is their combustion. A woman misreads her husband's instrumental aggression as expressive, searching in vain for the source and solution to his explosive irritation and, in so doing, placing increasing pressure on herself to modify her behavior. A man misreads his wife's expressive anger as an attempt to usurp his power in the home. Her catharsis is mistaken for challenge, and he reacts to that challenge as men have traditionally done: by counterattack.

Men, Intimacy, and Control

The central problem for abusive husbands is the same as that confronting most men in marriage: the interplay between their needs for both intimacy and control.[2] But in the abuser this problem is amplified and charged with vastly more significance. Raised to value autonomy and competition as cardinal virtues, men are expected to suspend these concerns in marriage in favor of intimacy and interdependence. Society has done a good job of teaching a man that he is superior to women, yet, in marrying, he must exchange his dominance for emotional equality. But to do this wholeheartedly, he must be certain that his wife is trustworthy. But what if she uses his powerless position against him? What if, like a man, she finds weakness instead of openness and uses that discovery to humiliate him? Most men take the chance and do not regret it. But the abusive husband cannot relinquish the nagging doubt that his dependence makes him vulnerable, and he uses aggression to reclaim control.

Aggression, whether verbal or physical, has a twofold advantage for men.[3] First, it distances the parties involved. Instead of partners, they are now antagonists. They discard empathy in favor of competition, and thus the relationship shifts from the emotional minefield of dependency to the more familiar male landscape of struggle for dominance. Winning and losing are the currency in which men have traded since boyhood; they are at home here. The second effect is the man's almost certain ability to win in any physical confrontation. No longer at his wife's mercy, thrown from power by the weakness of his love for her, he can take control in the arena he knows best.

For abusive men, the fear of intimacy and the assertion of power as its solution start in boyhood. One of the strongest predictors of wife beating by men is whether they were exposed to violence in the home as children.[4] Researchers have established that the boy who observes his father's violence is three times more likely to beat his own wife when he marries.[5] The boy learns that aggression pays. It puts an immediate end to arguments and restores order over the emotional clamor that has preceded it. His father gets what he wants: a freshly cooked meal, a tidy house, or, most important, a measure of deference by his wife.

That this deference results from her fear rather than her respect is a distinction of little significance to him. Like all boys, he is already well schooled in the playground hierarchy by which the most feared are the undisputed leaders, and the weak are disparaged as sissies and wimps. Whatever his parents may tell him about the "badness" of his own aggression, he has seen that violence works—especially on a smaller and less powerful victim. Wives are infantilized by violent husbands, turned from independent adults into naughty children whose misbehavior must be disciplined. One battered wife recalls how her husband systematically humiliated her in front of her children to demonstrate that she, like them, was subject to correction by the man of the house: "And this was 2 A.M. and he sat on the chair and sat and told me everything he thought about me and he dragged the full three kids out of their beds and made them all sit. He lined them right up against the couch and told them all what I was. He says to them 'Now you see her? She's a whore.' "[6]

But the boy does not simply identify with the aggressor. His love for his mother makes him empathize with her suffering, especially if he, like many such boys, has also been the victim of the father's violence. He sees that in his mother's and his own love for the father lie the seeds of their vulnerability. The terror and loneliness of their childhoods drive these men, as adults, to seek extreme and exclusive intimacy with their mates. This need for closeness and unconditional love is most apparent in the early stages of the relationship. It is easy, as one abused woman describes, to confuse possessiveness with passion:

> Ed and I did everything together during the first few months of our marriage. It seemed so wonderful, so flattering, to wake up in the morning with him next to me. We went shopping together and spent day after day just enjoying each other's company. Ed went everywhere with me and I went everywhere with him. I still did not understand that the closeness we were experiencing was so abnormal.[7]

But the intimacy that Ed and men like him need so desperately makes them vulnerable, just as their love for their fathers made them vulnerable. Sensitized to threat, such a man imagines he sees it everywhere: his wife is having affairs; she is laughing at him behind his back; she is more successful than he; she no longer loves him. Fearing her capacity to hurt him and to seize power in the relationship, he makes a preemptive strike that both distances him from her and ensures her obedience. Because we are all at our most vulnerable in the physical intimacy of the bedroom, it is here that men's fear of betrayal first takes root. A husband's vague suspicions crystallize into an obsession with his wife's immanent infidelity:

> One night, we had a party and I invited all of our neighbors. It was Bob's idea. He wanted to meet them all. We had people going in and

> out of our house all night. I knew I couldn't flirt with anybody, and I knew I could be nice but not too nice to them. But it didn't matter. Toward the end of the evening, two men who shared an apartment together came in and we offered them some drinks. I went in to the kitchen to get some ice and fix their drinks and one of them came in with me to help me. We were only a few minutes but when we came out, Bob started screaming and yelling at me that it took too long, that I was really having oral sex with this guy in the kitchen.[8]

Such jealousy is not only sexual but also extends to the wife's friends, family, and workplace—anyone who claims her attention becomes a threat to the husband's exclusive emotional ownership. A woman doctor describes how her husband became jealous even of the time she spent with her patients:

> We were supposed to go [to a hockey game] with a couple of his friends. I had a patient, and I didn't get home until close to 4:30. Mike was pacing up and down the floor when I walked in. I apologized for being late and told him that I was sorry but I could not leave this patient. We had had little incidents before but this was the first time I really began to be fearful. Mike's face started to get red, and I looked in his eyes and I became frightened. His eyes just looked like they belonged to someone else. His whole body began to change. It became more rigid and he started to yell at me. At first his abusiveness was really only about putting me down for caring about my patients and not caring about him.[9]

Obsessive jealousy on the part of a husband succeeds in effectively isolating his wife from other relationships. He increasingly controls her whereabouts, so that she rarely has even the opportunity to meet anyone. One woman described how she became virtually housebound: "We were two miles from the village. He allowed me half an hour to go up to the village and half an hour to walk back and ten minutes to get what I needed at the shops. . . . If I wasn't back inside that hour and ten minutes I got met at the door [by him] saying where the f———ing hell have you been?"[10]

Fear of betrayal is only one side of this version of house arrest. It also establishes, if there was ever any doubt in the wife's mind, who is in charge of the relationship. The simple choices that independent adults take for granted are denied to her. Moving about freely or engaging in conversations with friends or acquaintances becomes a luxury, not a right. As head of the household, her husband will decide whether she has earned these luxuries by her good behavior. One battered wife writes of the rediscovery of the most simple pleasure; she was "allowed" to walk down the street alone on a sunny spring day.[11]

But such privileges can be revoked at any time. And the enforced isolation has a more tactical and cold-blooded purpose: It prevents the woman from discussing the violence that is taking place in her home. For her husband's domination over her to be complete, there must be no possibility of her forming alliances that might curtail his ability to use the threat of force to control her. It is in an abusive man's doubt about his power that the real danger lies. Most men's sense of autonomy is bolstered by their jobs, their income, sports, and their social life. Assured of their worth in society, they are sufficiently confident to see little threat in their wives' occasional complaints or challenges. But abusive men tend to have low self-esteem and poor verbal skills and are prone to depression (as measured on standard personality tests).[12] Often they lack crucial resources outside the home that can confer status, such as money, education, social standing, and friends.[13] Thus any event that threatens their already shaky sense of status can be a trigger for the violence by which they mean to reclaim it. Job loss or chronic unemployment are especially powerful in reinforcing a man's lack of value in wider society, making him extraordinarily sensitive to being devalued in the home. This sense of inadequacy often goes hand in hand with drinking problems.[14] But, while many studies have noted that abusive men are more likely than nonabusers to drink excessively, the relation is not completely linear. The most extreme alcohol abusers among wife beaters are not the most violent men, probably because at very high dosages alcohol stupefies and such men lack the coordination or motivation for physical aggression. Broadly, however, there is a linear association between typical quantities of alcohol consumed per week and percentage of men who hit their wives. (To keep this in perspective, note that only 19 percent of the heaviest drinkers admit to striking their wives.) A national survey of couples that asked about involvement in domestic violence and alcohol use *at the time* of the last violent episode found, however, that in three-quarters of cases the man was not drunk at the time of the attack. But among the heaviest (binge) drinkers, 48 percent were drinking prior to the attack. The picture is complex but leaves little doubt that a drinking life-style is associated with spousal violence, even though wife beating is certainly not confined to the inebriated. Although wives often attribute their husbands' aggression solely to the effects of alcohol ("If he would stop drinking, he wouldn't do these things), research suggests that there is no direct pharmacological link between drinking and violence. Laboratory studies show that mere alcohol intake does not produce violence unless the drinker perceives some provocation. One major theory of alcohol abuse suggests that drinking increases concern with power among men, and that they often reinterpret neutral cues in the environment as hostile. When men drink in bars, they tend to be in the exclusive company of other men, and some writers have noted that wife abusers tend to spend a great deal of time with other men in patriarchal subcultures that highlight the importance of male dominance in the home. The confluence of concern with masculine power and an acute sensitivity to challenge may create a readiness to pick fights at home after drinking sprees.

Although each of these factors has been found to characterize male abusers, they represent the visible and extreme manifestation of a common underlying problem. Any man who feels himself losing control of his occupational or social life has the potential for violence. If he loses not only his acquired status in society but his ascribed status as head of the home, he may then develop a sensitivity to slights of the smallest kind and a preoccupation with his domestic rights and his wife's obligations. Any woman who has lived with an unemployed man knows how carefully she must bolster his ego, encourage his optimism, and avoid any imputation of failure. But even if he hears in her voice the suggestion of his inadequacy, the nonabusive man will limit his reassertion of power to sharp words or a moody retreat from the room. But if the wife of an abusive man refuses to accord the proper deference to him, the social etiquette of restraint meets a desperate need for respect at any price. The stage is set for violence.

Women, Stress, and Self-control

Because domestic violence is a major cause of injury to women—20 percent of emergency-room visits by women in urban areas are the result of physical abuse by their husbands[15]—we know a great deal about why men strike their wives[16] but virtually nothing about why women behave aggressively toward their husbands. If women's views of aggression involve a trade-off between stress and control, it follows that in the home either stress is high or control is low. Women in troubled or abusive marriages face an extremely high level of stress. But it is not only the "objective" amount of stress that is critical. It is the way the woman perceives, interprets, and defines the level of stress in relation to the amount that she can deal with. Some women can sail through episodes of interfering in-laws, faithless husbands, or colicky babies, while others go to pieces after the first disastrous dinner party. Equally there are differences in the extent to which women lower their control in the home. Some women accept from themselves nothing less than the "on-stage" behavior they display for the world, while others rely on the home as a place where they can let go and give up the confining self-consciousness that is demanded from them in other areas of their lives.

Let us look more closely at the stress factor in women's violence equation. We know that marriage is bad for women's mental health. Data show that married women have higher rates of neurosis and stress-related complaints than either married men or single women.[17] But why does marriage cause so much stress for women? The twin culprits are pressure and isolation.

Today the majority of married women work. But women's jobs are predominantly low-paid, low-skilled, and short-term,[18] hardly the "careers" we often read about in the popular press. Taking time off for children can lose a woman her job, and going back to work can mean a juggling act between baby-sitters and day-care centers. As they get older, she dreads school vacations and childhood illnesses. These considerations affect her working life—but not men's. Rarely will her husband take any responsibility for monitoring the complicated arrangements that parenthood requires. Back home, of course, the cooking, cleaning, and shopping still demand to be done, and, typically, working women spend twenty-six hours a week over and above their employment on these tasks. *Whether his wife works or not,* the husband spends eleven hours taking care of domestic business.[19]

For women who are not employed outside the home, the pressures may be different, but they are not necessarily less. Over 70 percent of housewives are dissatisfied with their lives.[20] Monotony is their main complaint. Their work neither requires nor holds their attention, so at no time can they be wholly involved in it. And there is no time off. As one woman put it: "The husbands never look tired, do they? It's always the woman that's tired, isn't it? When they've finished, they've finished. Things like digging roads might be harder than housework but there again when they've finished, they go and have a drink and a cigarette and that's it."[21]

One of the few areas of real decision making for a housewife is in budgeting. The daily management of money can become a powerful source of stress, however, if she is held accountable for household administration but deprived of the resources to deal with it effectively. In fact, money is one of the most common sources of marital arguments.[22]

Children also have the capacity to trigger stress-inducing arguments: Marital satisfaction declines in both partners following the birth of the first child and the early high levels are not recovered until the last child leaves home.[23] Not only are children an immense amount of physical work but they constantly demand attention. Their behavior, especially in the early years, can strain the patience of even the most devoted mother. There is precious little appreciation of her effort on the part of the children—or her husband.

> People just don't seem to understand how tired you get with two small children. From when he was five months Graeme never slept through the night. I thought that it was perhaps because he was cold—he used to wake up screaming as if in pain. The house was very damp with flaking patches, and I wanted to have central heating put in but Alan was very abrupt and aggressive—not "We'll talk about it" but "No, we can't afford it." Alan used to get annoyed if he was woken and I used to be in and out of our bedroom and the other

> room—the baby crying would wake the other one. If I could have brought the baby into bed with me he would probably have been all right but Alan wouldn't stand for that.[24]

Women are raised to be caretakers. It is by maintaining contentment in those around her that most women succeed in valuing themselves. Aside from the household work wives do for their husbands, they do emotional work as well. They tend to hold themselves responsible for their husbands' happiness.[25] When they fail, as they often must, women feel guilty. Apart from causing emotional exhaustion, this self-blame drives women to try harder and harder to improve themselves. As one battered wife puts it, "I actually thought that if I only learned to cook better or keep a cleaner house everything would be O.K. . . . I figured there had to be something *wrong with me.*"[26]

Women need to get out of the stress of the home and be independent people for a few hours if they are to refill the reservoir of caring that is constantly drained. But many wives dig themselves into a hole of social isolation by imposing upon themselves a moral obligation to spend most of their time at home.[27] The role of a wife (and even more of a mother) is to be available to her family. She is expected to be on call at all times. Even though her duties are not restricted to an eight-hour day (indeed precisely because her duties continue round the clock), she must make special arrangement to be absent from the home. The husband has responsibilities in the home too, but they are usually less arduous and clearly subordinate to his primary role in the workplace. And he is entitled to go out in the evening to recover from the stresses of the day, a right many women do not enjoy:

> He left me to do the garden too. His idea was to go to the pub on Fridays and football on Saturdays. He came home one Friday night, as I was up to my arms in [diapers] with the grass a foot high, and I burst into tears. He said "You always start a row just when I'm going out." I didn't want to stop him going out but I needed help.[28]

This woman's husband doesn't hear her cry from the heart, only an attempt to ruin his evening. If she were to go out herself and return to find that her child had fallen down or become ill, the accusation of her husband ("Where have you been?") would only reinforce the guilt she would feel about not being on call when she was most needed.* It is a rare husband who experiences this same sense of guilt: He may wish that he had been there to help, but he would not feel that his absence made him remiss in his duties.

The claustrophobia of the nuclear family is intensified by its isolation from the social support it so badly needs. Most women appreciate the wisdom of older relatives who can advise them about (and occasionally even relieve them of) some of the burdens of marriage and parenthood, while men are more likely to view this as uninvited interference.[29] But family members nowadays often live great distances from one another. And if parents become more distant after marriage, so do a woman's friends.[30] Although the husband may return to his old pattern of nights out with the boys, for the wife marriage often signals the end of evenings with other women. Especially in traditional working-class culture, they can be interpreted as opportunities for flirting with other men, particularly if the woman's friends are single. Her social life becomes limited to other married women, and their meeting places must be restricted to the movies or stores, for example, which offer no possibility of fraternizing with men. Some give up a social life altogether. One Englishman, abandoned by his wife, found out the hard way how isolating a woman's life can be and developed a "new sympathy for wives":

> [A]t least I manage to get out a bit. I've got two good babysitters. Some days when the children are out at school and the nursery and I've got my housework done, I can get up to the local [pub] and have a game of pool. My mates have been terrific. They've bought me a pint when I've been down. If I didn't go out, I'd go potty. But all women can do is sit in the house or talk to someone up the street. A woman can't go into the pub, not round here she can't, not without being called a whore or something like that.[31]

*Her feeling that the buck of emotional and physical well-being stops with her derives from and is maintained by the common social science habit of "mother blaming." In academic writing as well as popular women's magazines, it is the mother who is accountable for children's psychological adjustment, school performance, and social competence. When her children fail, she must assume the guilt more heavily than the father. (Sadly, when they succeed she less often receives the credit. She has, after all, simply done her job.)

As this man's comment shows, men's friendships revolve around *doing* things together. They go to sports events or to the local bar, and their conversations are a vehicle for playful rivalry and competition. Of course, women friends do things together too, but their friendships are much more focused on the exchange of emotion and experience. They are far more likely than men to talk about and analyze their marriages—and more willing to admit dissatisfaction. This knowledge makes many men see their wives' relationships with other women as threatening.[32] If they limit or forbid them, an important escape valve for women is lost.

It is not merely the opportunity to vent their own frustrations that women then miss; it is the perspective, the humor, the chance to feel part of a supportive network—to feel, even secondhand, a sense of involvement in the lives of others. If, deprived of this, a woman turns to her husband instead, she is likely to be disappointed. Most men cannot or will not openly share feelings of strain, insecurity, or depression.[33] They hear but do not listen, and they tend to rush for solutions before fully appreciating the problem. Men respond to difficulties by giving advice—easily confused with instructions by his wife. Directives about how to streamline her work load or reorganize her child care will only increase her tension. And it is a rare husband who can shed his ego sufficiently to listen to her problems without hearing them as nagging. Conversations that begin innocently enough on the wife's part as an occasion for getting things off her chest can turn in seconds into a screaming match. For husbands, as we shall see, there is a fine line between catharsis and complaint.

But what evidence is there that the domestic stresses I have described are related to women's aggression in the home? One important piece of data comes from a national survey in which stress was measured objectively by the number of traumatic events a couple had experienced in the preceding year, such as getting fired, being ill, or having a child suspended from school. The researchers plotted the relation between the amount of stress and the use of violence by husbands and by wives. They found that men's aggression rose in a fairly linear way as stress increased, but women's remained low until very high levels of stress were reached, then there was a dramatic upswing in their level of overt aggression. The researchers' graph is a visual testament to women's snapping point, which occurs suddenly at high levels of tension.[34]

A second piece of evidence comes from an examination of when verbal aggression between spouses escalates into physical violence. For women, being black and having a low income and low-status occupation were the most determining factors. For men, they were being black, having witnessed aggression as a child, and approving of the use of aggression. The author suggests that married black women "find it increasingly frustrating and stressful to deal with their mate's inadequate role performance" because of the high levels of unemployment among black men.

> Black men's aggressive behavior may be more *instrumental* perhaps to maintain control over their partner. Since black men grow up in an environment where aggression is accepted, they may learn to use it in order to possess power. On the other hand, black women's aggression may be more emotional in that it is an *expression* of their feelings of frustration or stress.[35] [Emphasis added.]

A third piece of evidence, to which I shall return in more detail in chapter 9, comes from studies of battered women who kill their husbands. What distinguishes them from other battered women is the degree of stress that is imposed on them by their mates, not a difference in their ability to tolerate it.[36]

These are some of the factors that can turn the home into an arena with high levels of tension. The other important contributor to women's increased aggression in the home is how the home diminishes women's usual self-control. The sociologist Erving Goffman has written eloquently of the front and back stages of social life.[37] According to him, when we are in the public eye we are like actors on a stage: We have a script to follow and a character to create for our audience. We carefully monitor our behavior, tailoring it to the requirements of our role and the particular drama we are enacting. But no one can maintain this level of self-awareness and control all the time. We all need to be backstage sometimes, where we can take off our makeup and relax. The home is the family's backstage.

Women are socialized to exert internal control over their anger, and this is reinforced by external control in public places.[38] The workplace is a veritable hothouse of frustration and stress,[39] to which is added, for women, the additional burdens of patronizing remarks, sexist insults, and sexual harassment. Yet women rarely lash out at their bosses or workmates. Although deviation from proper behavior can be enforced by the simple and brutal act of dismissal, it is not this fear but rather the ethos of the workplace, the understanding that we are in a front-stage region, that makes women control their anger and act out their nonaggressive roles so convincingly. But at home there is no audience, no critics. Inhibitions can be forgotten and the aggravation accumulated during the day discharged. If a woman comes home from work exhausted to find the breakfast dishes still unwashed or the television blaring to an empty room, suddenly the restraint she has imposed all day may evaporate. She can yell or throw something unhampered by her role of agreeable co-worker or caring employer. And, rightly or wrongly, many women do.

For most of us, the homes we grew up in are the only model of family interaction we know intimately. Some of us are raised in families where quarrels are a normal part of daily life. Others have been taught that displaying emotion is embarrassing and shameful. These patterns are associated with, but not determined by, culture and class.[40] Japanese and Italian families differ radically in their acceptance of open conflict, for example. Blue-collar families tend to accept higher levels of open verbal and physical aggression than do professionals.* Tolerance of physical aggression in the home also tends to be passed from one generation to the next.[42]

Over the span of a couple's relationship, from the initial heady romance to the more mundane cohabitation, there is often a progressive relaxation of standards. The woman and the man both become less concerned about putting on weight, dressing sloppily, and openly engaging in unpleasant habits. This same process of disinhibition increases women's willingness to express "uglier" emotions such as envy, depression, and irritation. When arguments erupt, the wife feels freer to use language and behavior that might once have shocked her husband. And conflicts themselves can shift the level of tolerable

*Violence in marriage is by no means confined to blue-collar families, but studies indicate a consistent relationship between lower socioeconomic status and physical aggression between spouses.[41]

aggression. Couples who frequently disagree may then have verbal fights, which in turn may lead to physical confrontations. Each time one partner escalates the extremity of violence, he or she defines a new and lower threshold for acceptable behavior, which affects the other; this is why, as mentioned earlier, in half of all abusive homes it is both partners who engage in violence.[43] Self-control is much easier to erode than it is to establish.

As we have seen, though, it is the stress of domestic life rather than a lowering of control that best accounts for women's aggression. Women take pride in their ability to cope with tension and, as some of the experiences of battered wives show, develop an extraordinary ability to maintain their composure and sanity through situations more reminiscent of a prison than a home. A woman copes because she feels that she has to—the home is her responsibility whether she likes it or not—and she has no right to indulge in emotional explosions. As stress slowly builds up, she habituates to it until it feels normal. But then something happens that may take her over the top.[44] It may be the first beating or something apparently trivial (such as a husband's condescending remark about her work), but for her it is the final straw. It is a short step to a showdown.

Collision Course

Few couples can honestly say they never argue. Many marital disputes, whether about money, vacations, or children, in fact grow out of a basic misunderstanding between men and women about the meaning of aggression. A man reads a woman's expressive aggression as instrumental, a bid for his power, and responds with aggression. She reads his aggression as expressive, an explosion of discontent with her and with their marriage. Her stress increases and she lashes out, trying to show how unhappy and desperate she is. He reads her anger as an attack on his control, and the cycle starts again. In extreme cases, this fundamental misunderstanding can begin an upward spiral that leads from anger to murder. But it begins with the kinds of domestic spats any married couple knows well.

When women are under stress, they want to talk about it.[45] For them, the tensions that build up during the day can be discharged at night when they sit down to share their feelings with a sympathetic listener. But what the woman sees as a chance to get things off her chest the husband can see as a competition or as an accusation. He finds no calm after the storm of another competitive day at the office and withdraws behind a newspaper. His wife, denied the chance to communicate with him, feels isolated and increasingly frustrated. She needs to vent her feelings yet when she tries to do so, she finds nothing but hostile silence or downright anger. Sometimes the loneliness and tension of these noncommunicative marriages can lead women to be the initiators of physical aggression. In incidents of mutual violence, women admit to striking the first blow in 42 percent of cases.[46]

> I knew Paul had been working very hard. He had this account and he had to get the work out for them or he might lose the account. . . . This was one of the biggest accounts the firm had and it was up to Paul to keep the customers happy. I had been alone night after night after night and I couldn't stand it anymore. I needed some companionship. Paul's tantrums and his weird behavior had made it so I couldn't keep any friends so I had no one to turn to. When he walked in that night at eleven o'clock the dinner was cold and soggy. I just pounced on him. I started screaming and throwing things. I know I shouldn't have done it. I know I should have kept my temper but I couldn't stand it anymore. I was just so alone. I thought, maybe he'll notice me. How can I make him notice me? I threw a glass and it hit his head and then went onto the wall and shattered. I then shoved a chair and caught him on the knee.[47]

In some marriages such an eruption may succeed in conveying the wife's message that she is at her wits' end and that she needs more time and support from her husband. If he is able to restrain his natural response to the attack, he might prevent future eruptions by meeting his wife's demands for attention. Men's customary reluctance to strike a woman may not extend to their wives, however. Marriage's relaxation of normal standards of behavior may make men respond to their wives first and foremost as people rather than as women. And there is the all-important factor of privacy. A man who would desist from aggression toward a female stranger in a bar might not show the same chivalry to his wife. With no audience to sanction his lapse from proper rules of conduct, the value of exercising his power when under threat could outweigh the social benefits of playing fair.

In most cases—about 58 percent—it is the man who first resorts to physical aggression.[48] Especially when things are not going well at work, he is acutely sensitive to any threat at home and may respond by asserting his physical superiority over his wife. This may be a threat to "shut up or else" or a push to get her out of his way. But push can turn to shove, and shove can turn to slap. The slightest thing can confirm his lack of power in the marriage. Male batterers often report that their wives' nagging is the chief source of their need to control them: "When my wife starts bitching it doesn't stop. She bitches about the kids, bitches about not being with the kids, bitches about too much work, bitches about me not helping enough. . . . There's no way to stop it."[49]

Not only husbands but even judges view such perceived nagging as a form of provocation by the victim.[50] But *nagging* has been cynically yet accurately defined as "continued discussion once the husband has made up his mind."[51] Failure to abide by his decision is apparently grounds for beating. Sometimes the "insubordination" comes from the wife's failure to cook her husband's food with sufficient care or to maintain the house to a high standard of cleanliness. It may also result from the belief that she does not love him enough or that his role as head of the household has been taken over by someone else:

> We were having a birthday party and my father was there. . . . Well I had my son blow out the candles and make a wish and then help make the first cut. I had him give the first piece to my father because he had to go to work. My husband stormed out of the house. . . . He came back loaded that night simply because my father had the first piece of birthday cake instead of him. . . . That was the first time he broke my wrist.[52]

Even more challenging than lack of respect from his wife is any attempt to compete with him economically or educationally. The suggestion that she might get a job or go back to school can be a powerful trigger for violence. But the most extreme provocation is his wife's decision to leave him—the final testament to his failure as a husband and to her betrayal of the intimacy that he demands from her. These incidents can be among the most violent of all marital conflicts.[53]

Women who are subject to very severe abuse by their husbands generally do not fight back, simply out of fear of the husbands' reaction.[54] But if his aggression is atypical or not so severe as to instill real fear for their lives, some women will retaliate:

> There was physical abuse right away. He would slap me a lot and I would fight back. Sometimes I didn't because I thought if I didn't it might cure him. I never started the fights, I mean physically. I just wasn't inclined to strike out at anybody ever. Then I tried striking back. I thought that might do it, that if I really fought back, he would straighten out; but that didn't solve it either. I think it made it worse.[55]

As this woman discovered, counterattack is not a very successful strategy for stopping a husband's violence.[56] Because men use violence to gain their opponent's submission and to demonstrate their power and control over them, a counterattack signals clearly that they have failed in this mission. They will tend to respond by striking back harder, setting in motion a vicious circle of escalating violence.

But if a woman leaves her abusive husband—often with no source of income and children in tow—her welcome with friends and relatives will quickly wear thin.[57] The response of acquaintances and neighbors is a curious blend of embarrassment and irritation. They do not want to be drawn into the conflict out of fear for their own safety and out of a belief that marital relations are private matters that a good wife does not discuss with others. In some cases they seem to be embarrassed by what they perceive as the wife's own embarrassment. But surely the parents of battered women would come to the aid of their daughters? Often the mother herself has been the victim of her husband's attacks and may have psychologically normalized them into an unpleasant but inescapable component of marriage. For his part, the father finds her presence an unwelcome reminder of his own culpability. At a purely practical level, the mother may not have the economic resources to take on the burden of extra mouths to feed, especially if the daughter has children. Doctors are often among the few who are privy to the wife's abuse, but in their role as healers rather than social workers their help is often limited to dispensing tranquilizers and offering encouragement for her to leave him. The police, until quite recently, have been unwilling to become involved in domestic violence. They responded to calls for service, but if the woman herself was the only witness and she is too fearful to press charges, they can only issue a warning to the husband. Many women are frightened to pursue a criminal case, sure that their husbands will take revenge when the police leave.[58] Even if she succeeds in her bid for an independent life, she may not have escaped continued violence. Separated women report higher levels of violence committed against them than do married women still living with their mates.[59] So threats by abusive husbands to hunt down their wives if they ever leave are not idle words, and many of them continue to harass, humiliate, and abuse long after their wives have moved out. Court orders of restraint are not merely difficult to enforce; they are downright provocative, because they signal yet another challenge to these men's control of their wives.

On the other hand, if a wife returns after a few days' or weeks' absence, the husband is often contrite—at first. In time, the beatings will no doubt start again. Tragically, many violent marriages culminate in murder, usually (in about two-thirds of cases) of the wife. Typically there have been numerous calls for assistance to the police before the fatal event.[60] Death threats are common—often including grim details of what he will do to her, what it will feel like, and how her body will look when he has finished.[61] These threats are most likely when a husband senses that his wife may be thinking about leaving him, telling others of his abuse, or having an affair. Beating, rather than the use of a lethal weapon, is the most common cause of death, and a man is far more likely than a woman to employ excessive violence—more than five separate acts to effect the murder.[62] Habituated to violence as a means of controlling his wife and maintaining self-esteem, her death is the final stop on a tragic journey from intimacy to isolation and from dependence to ultimate power.

When it is the wife who kills her spouse, studies consistently show that she almost always has a history of being abused by him.[63] One Chicago study found that all of the women in their sample had called for police assistance at least five times before the fatal incident.[64] In 60 percent of the cases where a woman kills her husband, *he* has initiated that violent incident. (This was true for only 5 percent of husbands who killed their wives.)[65]

The word *stress* seems inadequate to describe the emotional state of these women's lives. Not only are they beaten by their husbands but they often have no place to turn for sanctuary. Such women feel trapped and wholly at their husband's mercy. They learn to read the signals of imminent abuse and try harder to placate their husbands. But they are bound to fail, because the violence is not a reaction to what they do but a means of demonstrating power. Anything can be grounds for more beatings: silence is insolence; talking is nagging; retaliation is challenge. Women like Francine Hughes, whose tragic story is told in *The Burning Bed,* find that there is nothing they can do to appease and deter their husbands:

> First he'd play cat and mouse with me. For two or three hours he'd watch me as though he were daring me to do something wrong. I'd creep around cold inside with fear. If I sat and watched TV and the chair squeaked I'd look up quickly thinking that might be the thing that would start him. Then I'd look back at the TV so he wouldn't know I was afraid. He might get mad just because I flinched. Sometimes when he hit me I'd try to defend myself. It made things worse. If I ran out of the house Mickey would lock the door with a bolt so I couldn't get back in. I'd have to stay out there freezing or sitting in my car for an hour or so. When he calmed down he'd unlock the door. Then, if I was lucky, we could go quietly to bed. In the morning my face would be all puffy and purple. I'd put on makeup and go to school hoping no one would notice.[66]

The levels of stress to which this woman adjusted would be intolerable to most of us. When is the limit, even for her, reached? Angela Browne's study identified the common factors associated with abused women who kill their spouses: the frequency of their husbands' assaults, the severity of the injuries, the frequency of marital rape and other forced sexual acts, the frequency of the husbands' alcohol or drug use, the presence of murder threats against the wife, and the woman's own threats to commit suicide. Note that, of these, only one—suicide threats—is associated with the wife. The rest force her to exist in a state of permanent fear and anxiety, a state to which even her death may seem preferable.[67]

Yet these women seem completely unaware that the death that will take place will be their husbands' and not theirs. There is little evidence of its planning. Convinced that their own death or that of their child is imminent, such women have nothing left to lose:

> The next thing she remembers is being in the kitchen and the awful realization that another beating was starting. But she does not know why. Billy was wild—picking her up and actually throwing her against the walls, pounding her head on the stove and countertops, knocking her down, dragging her up and knocking her down again. Kim remembers holding her head down, trying to protect her face with her hands and saying, "Please, Billy! Please, Billy . . . Please stop! Please stop . . ." over and over. The next thing Kim remembers is standing in the living room facing Billy, putting a 7 mm rifle to her shoulder and firing once.[68]

It is very common for battered women who kill to have no clear recollection of the event.[69] The sheer power of their emotion drives them to actions whose consequences they seem to comprehend only dimly. Immobilized by disbelief, they rarely make any attempt to escape after the act. It is as if the anger has been so deeply buried and the accommodation to the husbands' violence so complete that it has erased any belief in the power of their own capacity to retaliate. When women kill it is an extension of the expressive aggression they have held in check for too long.

As the problem of extreme violence in marriage has become more well known, many programs have been put in place to treat abusive men by explicitly focusing on their preoccupation with control.[70] These programs attempt to change men's need for dominance into an appreciation that marriage is a partnership, not a dictatorship. These men must also learn that a woman who expresses unhappiness or irritation is issuing not a challenge but a plea for sympathy. Women in abusive relationships also need to own up to their feelings. It is easier for a woman to admit to fear than to anger, even when she has good reason to be angry. Too many women continue to believe that they have provoked their husbands' aggression, and that it is their duty to correct their behavior. Their restraint is read by their husbands as acquiescence to the abuse. Women who accept abuse as the price they must pay for marriage, who dismiss it as a temporary aberration, or blame it on alcohol unwittingly condone it and release their husbands from guilt.

At the other end of the spectrum, women who themselves use aggression not only increase the probability of becoming victims of their husbands' much more injurious violence but also provide them with a justification for it. Unless the causes of the stress are uncovered and solved, the pressure will build up until it explodes. It is possible in most marriages for women to talk about their frustrations without blaming the man. Simply announcing, "I need to talk some things out. Can you help me by listening? I feel like I'm bursting," can deflect a power struggle by making it clear that what follows is a plea for help. Men must learn to hear women as equals, and women must have an economically viable and physically safe way to make good on their promise to leave a violent home. It's a matter of life and death.

8

Street Gangs

THE image of the youth gang is one of masculinity and violence in their most extreme form. Standing on street corners in slums, clad in skull-emblazoned jackets, with sinister names like the Savage Nomads or the Devil's Disciples, gang members appear to be urban predators waiting for their next victim. They challenge and menace straight society. They define themselves by their opposition to the mundane, comfortable world of work, home, and family. Their hostility, their autonomy, and their social isolation epitomize and even caricature masculinity. By taking the meaning of maleness too far, they show us all that is destructive and cruel in it.

Despite this image, gangs are by no means exclusively male. Young women have been a part of them since the early nineteenth century,[1] and today girls comprise about 10 percent of gang members in the United States.[2] If the gang is the zenith of untamed masculine hostility, what attraction does it exert on young women? According to male researchers and boys in gangs, the answer is simple: Women want tough men and gravitate to gangs in pursuit of them.[3] Teenage boys are happy to boast about their sexual exploits with female camp followers. Regardless of what they actually feel about their girlfriends, they portray them as sexual objects, convenient but irrelevant outlets for the insatiable male libido. If the girls play any other role in gang life, according to the boys, it is as weapon carriers—since it is taboo for male officers to perform street searches on girls. From this perspective, these girls are marginal people—abused, exploited, and conned by the charismatic boys in the gang.

While male gang members merely extend masculinity into the world of criminality, girls seem to fly in the face of all femininity means when they fight in the streets. Social workers of the 1950s could think of nothing to do with them but teach them how to be "nice young women," conducting evening classes for them in cosmetics and sewing and teaching them how to shop in department stores.[4] Violence was seen as such an exclusively male enterprise that they believed effecting an Eliza Doolittle transformation would be enough to put an end to it.

It didn't. Girls continued to join gangs and to fight in the streets. In the 1970s their refusal to behave like ladies was given a contemporary academic twist. The rise in female crime (particularly violence by young women) was attributed to women's liberation.[5] As women achieved the same rights and responsibilities as men, it was argued, their behavior became more and more masculine. Or to put it another way, if women were taught their proper place they would stop committing crime and violence. Researchers took to the streets to measure the psychological masculinity of bad girls, with disappointing results.[6]

A fundamental mistake was made: The assumption that violence equals masculinity. In fact, it is quite possible for gang girls to have all the feminine qualities our stereotype dictates and still adopt an instrumental view of aggression. Social representations of aggression are freely available to us all, and our acceptance of an instrumental or an expressive view is a matter of the circumstances of our upbringing and the prevailing dynamics of our lives, not our chromosomes. So far I have made a straightforward equation of women with expressivity and men with instrumentality. But there are factors other than gender that can steer social representations.

Above all, representations must be functional. When they no longer assist people in their physical, social, or psychological survival, they will be abandoned. In explaining how female gang members come to adopt an instrumental perspective on aggression, we must look through these girls' eyes at the forces of threat they perceive. But first let's examine the more direct path taken by boys who wind up in gangs.

Masculinity and Gang Violence

Boys join gangs because at some level they actively seek out a self-image that includes violence. Being a hardman is an integral part of the attraction of the gang, and on average gang members are much more violent than other boys.[7] In Los Angeles in 1987 there were 387 gang-related homicides. Gang experts in that city have noted that gang homicide rates show five-year cycles of increase followed by a sudden drop. Even so, they add, "The cycles of gang homicide now seem to end with higher rates and retreat to higher plateaus before surging forward again."[8]

The increasingly lethal nature of gang violence is associated with the easy availability of guns.[9] Serious injury and death are obviously more likely when combatants are armed, and the vast majority of gang members admit to owning at least one illegal handgun. Back in the 1960s, gang violence was an event more talked about than real.[10] Hours of street-corner conversation fed upon rivalry with neighboring gangs, plans for rumbles, and fond retelling of much-embellished stories of past glory. Violence was about masculinity and honor, the establishing of group loyalty and personal courage. It was manifested mostly in fistfights and skirmishes involving taunts and threats of worse to come. The aim of these fair fights was to demean the opponent into submission and then walk away.

The presence of the handgun changed all that. The dividing line between an aggravated assault and a homicide is often a matter of luck. In most cases of homicide with a gun, the killer does not intend to kill. Usually a single shot is fired, and chance decides whether it strikes the victim's chest or leg. Now a victim felled by a shot in the leg presents a helpless and stationary target for a second bullet—yet it is rarely fired.[11] The point seems to be to discharge the weapon and thereby consolidate one's reputation as a hardman. So death, when it occurs, comes as a shock, even to the killer. The victimized gang swears revenge and, arming itself, makes a hit on the attackers. So begins a cycle of escalation that, however insane it may appear, follows its own hideous logic.

The violent image of the gang is a central part of its appeal. Gang members do not just need to belong to a group. If they did, the Boy Scouts or the local softball league would do as well. Gang membership is not just a proclivity to commit crime in groups. We know that teenagers all over the country prefer to commit their misbehavior with others—but they don't all join gangs.[12] It is not a professional crime organization. If it were, it would look like a junior Mafia, with secrecy and a determinedly low profile being the order of the day. The gang is a public celebration of violence. It proudly proclaims itself in its "colors," its insignia, its dress code, its tattoos, and the graffiti by which it claims ownership of a neighborhood. The hand signals gang members use to greet homeboys (fellow members) and identify rival groups, the preference for a certain color clothing, and the wearing of their hats tilted to one side or the other are all designed for public consumption.

The image of the gang is almost inseparable from that of the outlaw. Gangs whose members never commit crimes are simply not gangs. In refusing to accept the rule of law, gangs celebrate their masculinity and proclaim that they do not recognize any power greater than their own. They sneer at the police and return unrepentant from prison sentences, which represent a rite of passage to seniority in the group. They unite and blossom in the face of confrontation. Having little to believe in that significantly sets them apart from any other gang, they must rely on their hatred of other local cliques as their defining feature.

And gangs are acutely sensitive to their public image. (The gangs I studied in New York kept scrapbooks with clippings of newspaper stories about their exploits.) They enjoy being bad boys. One noted criminologist in Los Angeles, who worked with gang members for many years, actually warns against targeting social workers at any specific gang since other gangs resent the attention and may vie for equal recognition in violent ways.[13] Gangs clearly *work* at their notorious image. It is not a mere by-product of their criminal behavior or their group structure.

UNDERSTANDING THE MALE GANG

Each one of the three major theories of gangs faces difficulties in accounting for two crucial and interrelated facts about them: Their predominantly *male* membership and their consciously crafted *image of instrumental violence.*

The structuralist argument claims the gang results from economics. Western society shamelessly values material consumption as the ultimate index of personal and professional success. It reinforces the naive democratic message that all of us can make it if we really try, while carefully avoiding serious consideration of the lopsided distribution of educational and career opportunities that handicap the poor.[14] In response, teenagers accept the ends but not the means; they want the Mercedes but know they cannot get one by conventional routes. A recent variant of this approach focuses on the emergent black underclass in America.[15] With the opening of opportunities for talented minorities through affirmative action programs, the best and brightest have fled the crime-ridden urban scene. Those who remain feel like double failures. Lacking the skills to escape, they are mired in poverty, subsisting on welfare and the marginal and illegal economy. Little sense of neighborhood survives, and the social disorganization that results can offer no effective resistance to criminal predators. Gangs, in this view, are both a cause and a symptom of urban decay and poverty.

The social control argument focuses on the single-parent family, the deterioration and disarray of neighborhoods, and the failure of the school.[16] These are the primary instruments of socialization and control that keep young people in check. When control is eroded, antisocial behavior erupts. It is natural, primitive, and gratifying and is chiefly contained by surveillance.

The third theory, the cultural approaches, focuses on the social and personal symbolism of race or ethnicity.[17] Recent reports have considered Chicano gangs in East Los Angeles. Their existence and form are traced back to Mexican culture and its collision with American styles and values. Teenagers who are unable to assimilate into the American dream reassert their roots in forming gangs, which mirror the Mexican *palomilla* tradition of age-graded cohorts of peers. In their argot and dress, they express their *cholo* style—a pastiche of Mexican and American emblems and slang by which they resist the American way of life.

Women are curiously ignored in all three theories. Structural arguments focus almost wholly on classism and racism, but it is women, not men, who bear the brunt of the poverty that results. Any theory arguing that gangs are the result of economic inequality must surely predict that women would be at least equal partners in the roster of gang members. As for social control theory, women are also exposed to the erosion of family and community control, but they are much less likely to join gangs. Are we to believe that girls are inherently nicer than boys—that, when surveillance is lifted, natural human evil shows up less in them? The cultural analysis is both detailed and persuasive, but it explains only Chicano gangs. We need similar analyses for present-day Puerto Rican, Chinese, Vietnamese, and black gangs, as well as the Irish, Polish, and Italian gangs of the past. It seems singularly unlikely that gangs have been produced by totally distinct processes in each of these ethnic groups. During the course of the last two hundred years, the predominant ethnic makeup of gangs has altered time and again. What they all have in common is the gang as a predominantly male response to poverty and lack of opportunity. The culture that has to be examined is that of poverty-level and working-class masculinity.

And then there is violence. If the problems faced by gang members are structural and economic ones, then why do gangs not restrict their activities to robbery, burglary, and extortion? In what sense can violence solve poverty and joblessness? If gang violence were directed at white, privileged males, we might argue that it was a kind of primitive backlash, a form of political hostility based on what the gangs see as the unfair distribution of money. But gangs direct their violence at others like themselves in the surrounding neighborhood. Their victims are other minorities, usually other gang members. The social control approach has no means of explaining why the gang is formed at all. Why do we not see young people simply being delinquent in their own individual ways? And why, in the groups they do form, do they work so hard at developing a reputation for violence? The cultural approach, in pointing to the clashes in values and lifestyles between dominant and minority groups, does not directly address why violence should result. Surely minorities might equally well resort to separatism, alienation, repatriation, or assimilation.

MALE SUBCULTURES

The striking fact is that violence and resistance almost universally characterize young men at the bottom of the pecking order.[18]

Masculine youth subcultures share a defiance of and contempt for the bourgeois world. British sociologists have traced the trajectory of boys' high school careers as their grades and academic motivation plummet and they erect a barrier of contempt between themselves and the boys who succeed in school.[19] The good boys in England are the "earholes," in the United States the "college boys."[20] The bad boys are the "lads" or the "corner boys." They sneer at the anemic conformists, devaluing their success in the system as an effeminate desire to placate the school establishment. To reinforce their rejection of the system that has rejected them, they misbehave in the classroom, challenging their teachers' authority over them. The game is either to avoid lessons altogether (huddling behind school walls smoking cigarettes or marijuana) or, better still, become truant and pass the days in diners or pool halls. They dress to antagonize. In Britain, where school uniform is still required, they twist the rules by wearing their ties too low, their trousers too tight, or their hair too long. Across the Atlantic the same effect is achieved by sporting gold chains, gang jackets, or the "secret" colors of gang nations. Their posture and manner conspire to signal clearly that education represents an unwelcome intrusion into their real lives. They resist the system ritually or symbolically by being physically present while psychologically and socially absent. The message they send is simple: Education is the systems game, and we aren't playing.

Inherent in this refusal to grant authority to the school is another common thread of masculine youth culture: the superordinate importance of autonomy and self-determination. To conform is to play by someone else's rules and, by extension, to accept the role of follower. They must make it clear that no one can tell *them* what to do. Beyond the reach of conventional competition, they compete by asserting the value of autonomy over conformity.

But rejecting the establishment's game leaves one in danger of having no means at all to establish self-esteem and to assert one's worth over that of others. Because competition for power is so much a part of what it means to be male, some way must be found to establish who is top dog. Slicing through the middle-class and cerebral effeminacy of school life, gangs go straight to the heart of the matter—violence. Violence is power, and it is directed at other gangs and local youth because gang members want recognition and respect on their own turf. Violence is a measure of being someone in a world where all hope of success in conventional terms is lost. The dynamics of these lethal competitions for self-esteem have been described by the sociologist David Luckenbill:

> One begins by attacking another's identity, challenging his or her claim to a valued position in the situation. The other defines the attack as offensive and retaliates, attempting to restore identity either by threatening to injure the challenger if he or she does not withdraw or by using limited force to make the challenger withdraw. Rather than back down and show weakness, the challenger maintains or intensifies the attack. The opponents then battle. Fearing a show of weakness and a loss of face, and recognizing that peaceful or mildly aggressive means have failed to settle the dispute, one or both mobilize available weapons and use massive force, leaving one dead or dying.[21]

Gang warfare is this same pattern on a group level. Guns in hand, gangs make it a life-and-death contest. One researcher expressed it succinctly: "Worse than a no-good man is a sissy."[22] The boys in the gang take it one step further: "Better dead than a sissy."

Girls in Gangs: The Uses of a Reputation

The Sex Girls from Brooklyn, New York, are the female affiliate of the Sex Boys. Like most female gangs they are connected with a male group, though they have their own rules and organization. Booby and Weeza, two of its members, are sitting on a stoop sharing a joint and reminiscing about fights gone by: "This girl tells me, 'You'd better get out of here. This is my block.' I say, 'If you consider this your block, why don't you take me out? I'm staying right here, baby.' Then she sees me getting pissed off. She kept on talking to me. She got to the building then she ran upstairs. She wouldn't come down."

During the two years I spent hanging out with girl gang members, I heard dozens of stories like this one.[23] They sounded remarkably similar to the stories I heard from gang boys. All the same elements were in place: the claiming of the gang turf, the threat and counterthreat, the bravado, and the pride in scaring the opponent into submission. Clearly these girls were working on their reputations in just the same way the boys did. For the boys the swaggering functioned as a way of showing themselves to be real men. But where did this aggressive conversational posturing fit in to the girls' lives? Their concern with their appearance, their pride in their ability to attract men, their sense of responsibility as mothers left me in no doubt that they enjoyed being women. They didn't want to be like men and, indeed, would have been outraged at such a suggestion. I found the answer from a member of the Turban Queens:

> I'm glad I got a reputation. That way nobody will start with me, you know. Nobody will fuck with me—they *know*, you know. They're going to come out losing. Like all of us, we got a reputation. We're crazy, nobody wants to fight with us for that reason—you know. They say, "No, man. That girl might stab me or cut my face or something like that."

Fear and loneliness—in their families, their communities, and their schools—are the forces that drive young women toward an instrumental view of their aggression. They know what it is to be victims, and they know that, to survive, force must be met with more than unspoken anger or frustrated tears. Less physically strong and more sexually vulnerable than boys, they find that the best line of defense is not attack but the threat of attack. The key to this is the development of a reputation for violence, which will ward off opponents. There is nothing so effective as being in a street gang to keep the message blaring out: "Don't mess with me—I'm a crazy woman."

Most women see aggression as wrong because it threatens the relationships they hold most dear. But in the absence of these bonds, the door is opened to the use of aggression as a tool for distancing others. These girls fight to gain a reputation that will place a steel wall between them and the rest of the world. It effectively keeps out predators, but it keeps out intimacy and trust as well.

GIRLS AS VICTIMS

The fear and mistrust that propels them toward an instrumental view of aggression begins early for gang girls. Many come from homes where they see their mothers beaten and abused.[24] Weeza is in her early twenties and a founding member of the Sex Girls. She recalled her early years growing up in Puerto Rico:

> My father, he was always in the street—never bring money to the house. He used to work with smoke [marijuana]. He went to jail and everything, when we were small. When we got to about six or seven, he used to be going out, stay out, hit my mother. We always got to be moving, hiding, you know, late in the night and everything. My father used to come drunk, ask my mother for food. He never even bring no food to the house—no money. All hickeys over here, his shirt all full of lipstick. Sometimes I had to be running. Hiding. I say, "Shit, what kind of life is that?" He hit her one day with a stick. He brought some woman to my house when we was small. She stole two dresses from my mother's house in Puerto Rico. A whore on the street. My father took them to my mother's house.

Later Weeza found herself on the receiving end of her father's violence. She vividly recalled his anger when one of her friends refused his sexual advances:

> My father he was drunk and it was my girlfriend here. When he's sober, he's straight, but when he's drunk, he gets a little bit nasty. She don't want to pay no attention to him because she don't like him, so he just came to her and smack her. And I tell him, "You don't do that." That was in the street. Then she came up and he came up knocking on the door. My kid was here and he came to the living room and he start saying, "You're a whore," in Spanish and I tell him, "Look, stop that. This is my house. You don't do that in my house. She's in my house. You want to say that, you wait for her to go outside. Don't say that in my house because my kids are here." He told me, "You're another one." . . . But then he came in with a gun. He shot—he almost killed me.

Those girls who escape downright brutality may experience emotional rejection. Connie, the leader of the Sandman Ladies, saw her father die from heroin addiction when she was two. Her mother, in bad health and desperately poor, moved between New York and Puerto Rico, living with relatives or in run-down apartments. When her mother moved in with a man Connie hated, it was clear that either she or he would have to go. At the age of eleven, Connie was sent to live permanently with an aunt. The loss of her father and then her mother and the constant moves and disruption left Connie with the feeling that no one cared about her:

> I remember being so lonely, so lonely. Like an outsider. Like I didn't really belong because my father was the black sheep of the family. Here my aunt was stuck with this kid. From there I would go to my grandmother's house—my mother's mother. And I remember singing to her a Spanish song, "Who Is It That Loves Me?" I always used to sing that. I would always remember feeling so lonely, so lonely. By myself, by myself. Yea, I had all these people to look after me—to make sure I was well clothed and well fed—but I was alone.

When the earliest and most fundamental relationship of trust between a parent and a child is marred by violence, it becomes harder for the child to believe in the security of any relationship. As Weeza explains it: "I never think I was in love. Never. . . . I really don't know how to feel it. . . . Only my kids, I love them. But that's a different love." The bonds with their children are especially strong for gang girls. Because of the hardships they have known, they are extremely protective. And children provide a friend for girls who have come to distrust the world of adults. As one girl described her relationship with her baby daughter: "I think of her like a little sister in a way. And I say, 'Come on, you're little. You ain't got nobody else neither. You hang out with me and we'll learn these things together.' "

Though most vow not to tolerate the beatings they witnessed their own mothers suffer, history has a way of repeating itself. Physical abuse is so much a part of their romantic relationships that it is sometimes rationalized as a demonstration of love. Weeza explained how Misa, an ex-boyfriend, had intervened to prevent her from becoming a drug user: "He went and smacked me in front of the kids. He smacked me and told me, 'Look, you don't see how I live? I look like a dog, you know, like a junkie. I won't kick your ass because you're two kids are here.' "

The neighborhoods in which gangs thrive are among the poorest and most crime-ridden in the city. Burglaries and robberies are commonplace. Assaults in bars and on the streets are frequent. Drug dealers and pimps own the sidewalks. No one is safe there, not even a gang girl when she is walking alone—as Weeza found out one night when a group of men grabbed her:

> I said, "Please don't do nothing to me. I got kids." And they told me, "Shut up, shut up." So one of them put a chain to my neck—he kept pulling me to the empty building. It was dark, dark. He held me next to the wall with my throat and I said, "OK, I ain't going to scream." He told me, "Take your clothes off, I want pussy." I say, "No, no," but in the end he had me too tight and I couldn't talk. Then I tell him, "All right. I'm going to take my clothes off. Let me loose. I ain't going to scream or nothing." Then when I push him, I ran.

In the context of the routine violence that surrounds them, the attraction of the gang for such girls is not hard to see.

GIRLS AS CRAZY

The girls' gang offers solutions to two fundamental needs: acceptance and safety. It is a sisterhood of like-minded others and an escape from victimization by sheer force of numbers and a tough reputation. But girls must gain entry through an initiation ceremony. Far from deterring prospective members, it encourages them. Initiation guarantees an exclusivity and kudos to membership not unlike that of sororities or country clubs. The gang will not accept just anyone, and this fact alone augments the members' self-esteem, which has taken such hard knocks from teachers, social workers, police, and families. It also guarantees that members will be willing and able to fight in support of one another. This give-and-take of protection and support is what initiation is all about. The gang rejects "prospects" whose aim is merely to avail themselves of the gang's fighting ability for their own ends:

> Like there's some girls who want to join who think, "I get in trouble, I got backup." Now for us, this wasn't it. We used to take a new girl to the park. Now that girl had to pick one of our girls. And whoever she wanted, she had to fight that girl to see that she could take the

punches. Without crying. . . . Like if I'm walking down the street with you, you have to be able to count that I'm going to throw my life for you. Just like I expect you to do it for me. I have to be able to say, "I'm going to stay here and fight because I know you're going to stay here and fight too."

The demonstration of "heart" or courage in the public forum of intergang feuds is a requirement for the image-promoting talk that the girls enjoy. Once a girl has proved that she is capable of handling herself in a fight, she is licensed to proclaim herself a "crazy bitch." This mutually endorsed bragging is a process by which specific acts of daring are stylized, elaborated, and offered as incontrovertible evidence of toughness. Stories are told and retold; each time the fear is minimized and the cold instrumentality exaggerated, until the girls convince their listeners and themselves that they are invulnerable. Connie, at the ripe old age of twenty-eight, was a practiced raconteuse:

I had to fight with a chick, and I had my .25 automatic and I had my switchblade. I mean I was put on the spot. The thing is whenever the spotlight is on me, I'll always try to do my best. Because I don't want to come down. So you take the biggest one and you make the best of what you're going to do. Like the way I see it is, once you get up, you're going to be arrested anyway. If you leave her dead, leave her dead. Just grab one and the way I'm going now—I'm going for the eyes. I feel if I'm going to jail anyway, I'm going to make the best job of it.

Such ruthless bravado helps reassure these girls of their own fearlessness, and they begin to use aggression preemptively, as a response to any potential threat. Connie described an event many urban women have faced, to which she responded with her own gang-nurtured craziness:

This morning I'm walking with Suzie and this man comes up and I hear him say out of the clear blue sky, "Come up to my apartment." So I look at him and I say, "How in hell is he going to have the nerve to come up to me and think I'm a whore?" So I took out my knife and I went *flick*, and I jumped at him and he jumped back. I said

> "Come on, mother———, say it again. Come on. Come on." He said, "No, you think you're so bad. You're the woman with the knife. You come over here." And I said, "No. You're the one who ran, why don't you come back?" Then he said something about, "You should stick that up your ass." I said, "You're man enough, why don't you come over here and let me stick it up your ass?" And he just kept on walking. Because he knew that if he had come over, I would have stabbed him. It was vibrating from my body.

This situation held no immediate danger. Connie, like most of us, could have pretended that she didn't hear and simply walked on. But Connie is acutely sensitive to threats because they reawaken memories of the exploitation and impotence of her childhood. Producing a knife signals her craziness. The man gets the message loud and clear. And Connie proves to herself and him that she is in control.

Many of the fights that gang girls are involved in are about romantic jealousy. When they discover that a partner has been unfaithful, the reaction follows a violent logic. Men, as they see it, are incapable of turning down an offer of sex, no matter who the girl might be. Besides, the men have their reputations to consider: How would it look to their fellow gang members if it became known that they had turned down a sexual proposal? From the gang girls' point of view, this means that any woman who comes on to a man must bear the full weight of responsibility for his infidelity. She has committed two unforgivable sins: She has tried to injure them emotionally by taking away one of their few intimate relationships, and she has insulted their tough reputation. A member of the Turban Queens describes the swift retribution that follows:

> I would just go up "Hey, I hear you made it with my old man." And blat! The whole thing is over because they don't even raise their hands. They put their head down and they cut out fast. Because they know, if I was hitting a girl and they hit me back and all these girls see it, they're going to get in. And she's going to take a worse beating. So she takes a slap or two and goes home and cries.

The boyfriend is an emotional possession, and the dispute is over ownership and control. The rhetoric in which gang girls frame the issue is typically masculine: "Don't humiliate me by trying to take what is mine." It is in stark contrast to an expressive representation of the same situation, in which, if violence were to occur, it would probably be directed toward the boyfriend to show him the pain and anger he had caused. But gang girls have seen that patience and forbearance led their mothers into abusive and empty marriages. The other woman has to be stopped if they are to hold on to their man and their self-esteem.

Fear and Survival

So hard do gang girls work on their crazy reputations that it is easy to miss the small voice of fear and vulnerability that runs as a counterpoint to the brave talk. Booby's description of the value of toughness reflects the fear of its opposite:

> Let's say you're a new jack round here, right? You be going to the store, they be taking your money. Now if you ain't going to kick their ass, they're going to keep picking on you. So before they wind up kicking your ass, you got to get tough on them. If not, you can't even walk the streets by yourself. They're going to wind up hurting you or killing you or whatever they feel.

Yet even for girls who have learned that lesson well, the moment of confrontation still brings fear. Each new fight holds the possibility of defeat and, with it, vulnerability—for others might hear that they are an easy target. This drives them forward to more fights and a greater sense of their own inviolability.

> I always get nervous even when I'm just arguing with somebody. There's times when I see a real big girl that I get scared. I think, "Damn, I'm going to hurt her or she's going to hurt me." But once you're in a fight you just think, "I've got to fuck that girl up before she does it to me." You've got to really blow off on her. You just play it crazy. That's when they get scared of you.

The transformation from fear to belligerence is essentially a shift from an expressive to an instrumental representation of aggression.

Self-control and the containment of anger do nothing to prevent victimization. So they begin to see aggression as a way of controlling other people. It becomes instrumental.

But boys in gangs eagerly exploit the full range of their instrumental aggression. They use it not just for gaining social recognition but for criminal ends. They hire themselves out as bodyguards, use violence to keep other potential drug sellers out of their turf, rob, mug, and extort money from local businesses. Violence pays, materially as well as socially. Girls in gangs are far less involved in these kinds of money-motivated crimes of violence. Aggression in their lives is a means of survival. Reputation is about preventing victimization, not about flashing a wad of bills.

Secure in our relationships and relatively protected from physical harm, most women do not need to use aggression as a tool to keep the world at bay. But when the ties that bind women close to others are destroyed, what do they have to fear in aggression? They cannot fear the loss of what they do not have. And the indisputable law on the street is fight or get beaten. The reasoning that leads women to this instrumental use of aggression is not confined to the gang. Wherever women face lives of brutal exploitation that destroys their faith in the value of trust and intimacy, they will be driven to it. We cannot demand that women desist from its use when their survival requires it. We should demand instead that the trust and dependency of young girls be respected and rewarded rather than turned against them.

9

Women's Aggression and the Male Establishment

THE most frequent target of women's anger is men, because it is they who impose their will most strongly over women and are often the cause of women's frustration. But actual violence by men against women is a line of last resort used only when power is under threat. Hannah Arendt has written: "Power and violence are opposites; where the one rules absolutely the other is absent. Violence appears when power is in jeopardy, but left to its own course it ends in power's disappearance."[1] Violence is a relatively rare event because, in the daily running of life, power is exercised by men in far more subtle and effective ways than by brute force. Paradoxically, the most effective form of power disguises itself in such a way that it is all but invisible. This is what has been called the "third dimension of power"—the sleight of hand by which oppressors hide oppression from the view of the oppressed.[2]

Yet most women feel it almost imperceptibly on the outskirts of their consciousness, there in the taken-for-granted facts of life. We can't go to college right now because we have to support our husbands. We must remain bored and unfulfilled at home because, we are told, our children need us there. We cannot expect to be president because a woman could never make it. We must organize the dinner party for his boss because socializing will be good for his career. As the sociologist Steven Lukes eloquently puts it: "Is it not the supreme and most insidious exercise of power to prevent people, to whatever degree, from having grievances by shaping their perceptions, cognitions and preferences in such a way that they accept their role in the existing order of things, either because they can see no alternative to it, or because they see it as natural and unchangeable, or because they value it as divinely ordained and beneficial?"[3] For centuries women have had their anger hidden from them by their belief in the naturalness of their subordination and their acquiescence to men. How could they presume to be frustrated when they have a home, a loving husband, and beautiful children?

But many women have recognized that something is wrong. They struggle to leap the barrier of the third dimension of power, and, as they do, their discontent becomes visible to them. A new strategy of control is needed to contain them, more overt than the last. Men retain the power to set the social agenda.[4] They can decide which items are worthy of consideration. They can deny women's right to have their voices heard by refusing to recognize their grievances as real. We can see this in small issues in the home as well as in major decisions in the boardroom. Sheila, an art teacher and mother of two, wants to set up her own graphics business. For years, she has gone through the motions of teaching, but her heart is no longer in it. She is still young enough to make a new start. As she discusses her plan, her husband nods. He suggests that she postpone it—perhaps until the children are older and child care will no longer be a problem. He points out that she has managed quite well up to now, surely a few more years wouldn't matter. Ignoring and minimizing potential grievances keep the issue from being either acknowledged or dealt with.

When denial fails to silence a woman's grievances, the next level of power is often used—the power to define the issue in male terms. A woman who expresses anger to a man finds that her actions, which for her are a legitimate expression of frustration, are reinterpreted. She is "not herself" and needs to calm down, take a tranquilizer, or even seek therapy. Or she is issuing a direct challenge to him, using her aggression instrumentally to seize power away from her husband: a bitch.

These three forms of control over women's aggression—concealment, denial, and redefinition—are visible between husbands and wives as well as in social institutions. The distribution of power in our society places men in key decision-making roles. As elected representatives, legislators, policy makers, and law enforcers, they are the agents of social control in almost all spheres of life. They regulate and determine what is seen as a threat to society, who is bad or mad, who is to be locked up, and who is to be treated. As they make these decisions, they do so as trained experts in their fields but also as men. For years, the institutions these men run have helped make women's aggression invisible, an ugly little secret that even women could barely see. A husband contained his wife's aggression in the privacy of the home, hiding it from neighbors and making the woman herself deny it. Delinquent girls were far less frequently prosecuted than boys for acts of aggression, instead being returned to their parents to be silently controlled in the home. Research on aggression used only male subjects because women simply were not seen as aggressive.

But by the 1970s and 1980s, women's aggression had become harder and harder to ignore. Female criminologists began to write about this taboo subject, and national surveys revealed women's high level of aggression in the home. Instead of putting a spotlight on the new findings, however, these uncomfortable events triggered the minimization phase. Men preferred not to dwell on women's aggression because it was an ugly sign of potential resistance. Women's groups colluded with them; to recognize its existence would draw attention away from men's far more lethal aggression as well as highlighting undesirably assertive qualities in a group they wanted to depict as victims. Most violent offenders were men, so women's aggression was not a serious social problem. It could be studied as a curiosity, an aberration, characteristic of very few women but not weighty enough to join the mainstream of the social agenda.

Aggressive women have always run the risk of being stigmatized as harridans, shrews, and viragos. But we see now more than ever a formal shift toward redefining women's aggression in male terms. I have discussed throughout this book how men and women hold different representations of the meaning of aggression, but they are far from equal in their power to make their own representations stick. We need to examine the consequences for society of a masculine professional elite that holds an instrumental view of aggression. I do not mean to imply that there is an orchestrated male conspiracy against women, but rather that injustice and misunderstanding will inevitably occur when one powerful group tries to force its interpretation upon another group whose behavior defies explanation in those terms.

When men sit in judgment over other men, their dialogue with one another is at least conducted within the same rhetorical framework, even if the role of one is to evaluate the other. Terrorist bomb setters, armed robbers, hostage takers, rioters, youth gang members—their actions make sense within an instrumental understanding of aggression, aimed as they are at achieving social ends, whether political change, monetary benefit, or a reputation as a hardman. Their violence is judged to be legally and morally wrong, but it is at least comprehensible. But faced with female aggression, the system finds itself at a loss. Male judges—both the official ones in the law courts and the unofficial moral entrepreneurs in the media—try to place a masculine and instrumental interpretation on women's behavior. Sometimes the fit is good, as in the case of a woman bank robber or political terrorist. Other times, as with an abused wife who turns on her tormentor after years of victimization, the law is determined to view her action as instrumental even when the weight of the evidence strongly suggests otherwise. But the price for the woman is high. Her actions are forced into a masculine model of aggression, judged to be male, and the woman is seen as having violated not just the criminal law but the "natural law" of proper female behavior.

But there are occasions when female aggression steadfastly refuses to bend to a straightforward means-ends analysis. In the minds of many men, female aggression remains shrouded in mystery—capricious, irrational, arbitrary. If it cannot be explained in "rational" instrumental terms, then it cannot be explained at all; violent women must be either trying to be men or just crazy.

To illustrate this process, I have chosen three diverse arenas in which male institutions have exercised control over the explanation for aggression by women—and in so doing torn away women's right to their own understanding of it. I begin with the extreme case of women who kill, then move on to the dangerous psychiatric labeling of aggressive women and the controversy of premenstrual syndrome.

Battered Women, Murder, and the Law

The vast majority of homicides committed by women are of their husbands or lovers, specifically those who have physically abused them. In recent years, women charged with this crime have experienced a collision between their own understanding of their aggression and that of the male-dominated criminal justice system.

The law distinguishes between two levels of lethal violence: murder, in which there is a clear intent to kill or to injure seriously without legal justification or excuse; and voluntary manslaughter, where the same intent is partially justified because it is committed under provocation from the victim and in the heat of passion. It might seem that any battered woman who kills her abuser could only be charged with manslaughter, since her history of victimization obviously indicates provocation by the victim. But in fact many women are charged with murder because manslaughter's "heat of passion" component requires virtually no delay between the act of provocation and the killing. The law is geared to the archetypal situation of infidelity where a man discovers his wife in flagrante delicto. Any time delay between the provocation and the killing opens the door to the motive of revenge, which changes the stakes considerably.

Now there is no reason for a husband to delay in exacting retribution. But a battered woman faces a very different scenario. After enduring years of abuse, she is once again battered by her husband. Exhausted and physically injured, she is in no position to retaliate. He goes to bed. She sits on the floor crying, confused, sensing that no matter what she does, he will always beat her. Finally she realizes that her own tolerance of the beatings is not heroic but cowardly. Rather than cooling down, she maintains or even increases her anger by remembering every punch, her powerlessness in the face of it all, the failure of the police or friends and family to prevent it, and her husband's threat to kill her if she tries to leave.[5] She picks up a gun, walks into the bedroom, and fires it into his sleeping body. Hours have probably passed since he struck her. In the case of abused wife Kiranjit Ahluwalia, the law acknowledged that after an abusive incident a woman's anger might increase rather than decrease as time passed. Nonetheless it held that the longer the delay, the less plausible a defense of provocation became. Her motive, in the eyes of the law, is not provocation but revenge. The charge is murder.

Because the law is geared to the idea of a single provocative act and an immediate retaliatory response, many judges deny the female defendant the right to introduce evidence of continued beatings in order to support her defense of provocation. They argue that her history of being battered is irrelevant; it suggests only that she tolerated it for a long period of time without reacting in the heat of passion. To quote one judge's assessment, "the further removed an incident is from the crime, the less it counts."[6] There is an astonishing irony here: A woman who controls her anger for months or years is deemed to be incapable of anger at all.

To deny the relevance of prolonged abuse to the increasing level of a woman's anger is to deny the very basis of a woman's expressive use of aggression. It effectively punishes her for failing to lose her temper quickly enough. It is vital to see the violent act in the context of the abuse that preceded it, the impotence of the justice system to remedy the abuse, and the woman's feelings at the time of the killing. Without this information, a jury simply cannot accurately appraise her state of mind or her actions. But a jury may never learn of the events that took place prior to the killing.

The time lag between the provocation and the reaction dominates all other considerations in a provocation defense.[7] Consider this newspaper item:

> MAN PROVOKED INTO KILLING
>
> A man who killed the bullying, alcoholic woman with whom he lived was given a suspended two-year jail sentence yesterday. . . . On 27 February when he returned home to find her drunk and demanding more drink, he kicked her. She died from internal bleeding. Malcolm Morse, for the prosecution, said "It was a sudden temporary loss of control caused by provocation." Passing sentence, Mr. Justice Popplewell told McGrail: "This woman would have tried the patience of a saint."[8]

As this case shows, the "heat of passion" argument apparently overrides consideration of both *degree* and *duration*. Sara Thornton and Kiranjit Ahluwalia attracted widespread publicity and sympathy for battered women's plight. Both women killed their husbands after years of abuse but did so when their husbands were asleep. No one doubted the suffering their husbands had inflicted on them, but the time delay between the last beating and the killing made them both guilty of murder in the eyes of the law. Unlike Mr. McGrail, they were sentenced to life imprisonment. In admitting evidence of sustained abuse, much more emphasis needs to be placed on whether the abuse was verbal or physical and on its severity, including testimony by witnesses and doctors. And to do justice to women's self-control, information should be given on how long the woman in question had tolerated the beatings. Rather than showing that she did not object to it or even enjoyed it, cumulative violence should rightly be seen, as one legal scholar has said, as leading to cumulative rage.[9]*

If judges are unwilling to consider seriously a woman's history of victimization, juries are strongly influenced by it—as demonstrated by their refusal to convict for murder when such evidence is introduced. In Great Britain, where a conviction for murder carries a mandatory life sentence, juries may be more inclined to reach a verdict of not guilty simply to avert this draconian sentence. Their tendency not to convict in these cases may also be related to their commonsense understanding of the term *provocation,* which boils down, in many people's minds, to the question, "Did the victim ask for it?" In cases of spouse murder after prolonged wife abuse, the answer seems to be yes.

A finding of provocation, as I explained, transforms the killing from murder to voluntary manslaughter. Self-defense, however, results in full exoneration. Yet in the United States, despite the fact that 87 percent of women who kill their battering husbands believe they acted in self-defense, many are still convicted of murder or manslaughter.[10] Jennifer Patri shot her husband when he came at her with a knife. Joyce Hawthorne shot her husband while he was choking her. Betty Ann Harrison stabbed her batterer as he pulled her back into the trailer where he had just beaten and attempted to rape her. All of these women were convicted in spite of self-defense pleas.[11] So uncertain is such a plea that some defense lawyers advise their clients to plead down to manslaughter rather than fight a murder charge with self-defense. Gloria Timmons was raped, beaten, and scalded with boiling water by her estranged husband. While she was in the hospital recovering from injuries sustained when he threw her down a flight of stairs, he arrived at her bedside and beat her again. While awaiting trial for this attack, he came after her yet again, this time with a screwdriver. She shot him. To avoid the

*In New South Wales, Australia, an act was passed in 1982 that allows for the introduction of information about any past conduct of the victim toward the defendant as relevant to the issue of provocation. The events occurring immediately prior to the killing are deemphasized in favor of closer scrutiny of the cumulative impact of abuse.

possibility of a failed plea of self-defense, she agreed to plead guilty to manslaughter. In Great Britain, not one plea of self-defense has succeeded among women who have killed their abusive husbands.[12] To understand this phenomenon, we need to examine what such a defense entails.

According to the law, a person may use deadly force against another only in the *reasonable* belief that the other presents the threat of imminent death or serious bodily injury and that deadly force is necessary to avert the infliction of such harm. The stumbling block has been the notion of "reasonableness." Until recently, the archaic wording of "reasonable man" was retained, but even after it was changed there was no specific provision for women's point of view to be considered. The law is becoming sensitive, however, to the need to consider perceptions and judgments other than those made by white, middle-class males. In the 1977 case of Yvonne Wanrow, who wounded one man and killed another whom she believed to be child molesters and rapists, the Washington State Supreme Court held that the "reasonable man" jury instruction potentially denied women equal protection under the law. The court decided that

> the respondent was entitled to have the jury consider her actions in the light of her own perceptions of the situation, including those perceptions which were the product of our nation's long and unfortunate history of sex discrimination. . . . To fail to do so is to deny the right of the individual woman involved to trial by the same rules which are applicable to male defendants.[13]

This decision was crucial in focusing attention on the specifics of what seemed reasonable to a particular woman faced with such circumstances. But many states have resisted the decision because, they argue, it places too much emphasis on individual differences in perception and suggests a shifting and unreliable application of the standard of self-defense. Yet perhaps a middle path can be found by requiring that the woman's actions be those that would be taken by *any reasonable woman* faced with such a situation—including any abuse that led to it. This would acknowledge differences in size and strength between the parties and also the fact that gender affects our understanding of events and hence the reasons behind our conduct.

Clearly, the reasons a woman commits domestic homicide are distinctively different from those of a man. His action is the extension and culmination of continued physical abuse in which his failure to satisfy himself of his power over his wife results in a fatal increase in force. He kills in an attempt to make her behave with proper deference. Her action is a result of being driven to lose self-control by repeated beatings. She kills to make the madness stop.[14] Yet the former is apparently more "reasonable" than the latter, according to statistics that show proportionately more wives than husbands being convicted of spousal murder. As two attorneys, Elizabeth Schneider and Susan Jordan, have pointed out:

> Standards of justifiable homicide have been based on male models and expectations. Familiar images of self-defense are a soldier, a man protecting his home, family or his wife, or a man fighting off an assailant. Society, through its prosecutors, juries and judges, has more readily excused a man for killing his wife's lover than a woman for killing a rapist. The acts of men and women are subject to a different set of legal expectations and standards. The man's act, while not always legally condoned, is viewed sympathetically. He is not forgiven but *his motivation is understood* by those sitting in judgment upon his act since his conduct conforms to the expectations that a real man would fight to the death to protect his pride and property.[15] [Emphasis added.]

The law of self-defense is about reason, and particularly about masculine reason in the face of threat. It assumes that the action taken is instrumental toward the specific goal of incapacitating the attacker. Emotion would disrupt the process of reason, and the necessary absence of passion is summed up in the requirement that the force used be proportionate to the degree of threat implied by the attacker. Deadly force is to be used when the attacker threatens death, lesser force when the attacker is unarmed. These kinds of assessments come automatically to most men, trained as they are in the rules of fair fighting and the containment of extreme emotion in the service of the instrumental use of aggression.

But women have been schooled in the containment of aggression. They have learned to fear their own violence and, in the face of an attacker who is stronger, heavier, and taller, are particularly unlikely to fight back. More important, theirs are not one-shot encounters between equal adversaries governed by rules of fair fighting. Most battered wives have sought to escape their husbands' abuse through shelters, court orders, criminal proceedings, or divorce. But many men simply will not give up. Their determination to pursue their wives and their threats to kill them if they go to the police conspire to keep many women in the most dangerous of all places: their homes.

The twisted reasoning of the prosecution will claim that she had survived many previous beatings by her husband, so why did she expect that the attack would be fatal that time? (Of course, the logical extension of such an argument is that a woman cannot plead self-defense unless she is killed.) A husband may, as many battering husbands do, announce, "Next time, I'm going to kill you," but the burden of proof is on the woman to show that the words were spoken in earnest and that she had reason to believe that the "next time" was imminent. The effect of the beatings and the threats is to produce an atmosphere of enormous, unremitting tension from which there seems to be no escape. Two psychiatrists experienced in treating battered women vividly describe the rising level of stress and tension that can ultimately explode into expressive violence:

> [T]he stress was unending and the threat of the next assault ever-present. . . . Agitation and anxiety bordering on panic were almost always present: "I feel like screaming and hollering *but I hold it in.*" "I feel like a pressure cooker *ready to explode.*" They talked of being tense and nervous by which they meant *"going to pieces"* at any unexpected noise, voice or happening. Events even remotely connected with violence, whether thunder, people arguing or a door slamming, elicited intense fear. . . . Any symbolic act or actual sign of potential danger resulted in increased activity, agitation, pacing, screaming and crying. They remained vigilant, unable to relax or sleep.[16] [Emphasis added.]

The killing, when it occurs, is far removed from a cold assessment of the level of force reasonably needed to avert the next attack. It is a cataclysmic explosion of stress, frustration, fear, and hatred.

Perhaps, then, the most appropriate defense for the woman is one of temporary insanity. But that would leave the male-centered law of self-defense untouched and render any woman who does not behave like a man crazy. And if she is crazy, then so is half the human population, since she has behaved as many other normal women would if faced with such a pathologically abnormal situation. Of the three parties to the affair—the woman, the battering husband, and the legal system—it is certainly not the woman who is crazy. Kiranjit Ahluwalia suffered almost daily abuse for the ten years of her marriage. On appealing her murder conviction, the judge refused to reduce her conviction to manslaughter because of her husband's provocative behavior.[17] He did, however, grant her a retrial for manslaughter based on evidence that she was suffering from diminished responsibility (temporary insanity) at the time of the killing. She pleaded guilty and was sentenced to time served. In Liverpool Sandra Fleming shot dead her partner after ten years of torture, mutilation and sexual abuse. She was freed on probation not because she finally reacted to the "life of misery and horror" which the judge acknowledged she had endured but because she claimed diminished responsibility. Insanity has been a woman's best bet in terms of a defense. Courts find it easier to label such women mad than to challenge the androcentric law that refuses to acknowledge women's distinctive experience of anger and response.

Insanity has been a woman's best bet in terms of a defense. Courts find it easier to label such women mad than to challenge the androcentric law that refuses to acknowledge women's distinctive experience of anger and response.

To date, the contribution of psychology has been in terms of expert testimony on the "battered-woman syndrome." Leonora Walker used the theory of "learned helplessness" to account for battered women's remaining in the home.[18] Coined by the psychologist Martin Seligman, the term described the apathetic behavior of dogs subjected to random electric shock they were unable to control. When then placed in situations where they *could* escape the shocks, the dogs did not do so.[19] The problem is that the expert testimony aptly describes why the woman fails to escape from the home but not why she turns on her attacker and kills him.[20] Indeed, the fact that she does indicates that she is far from helpless. Also, the idea of a "syndrome" tends to imply a psychological disability, which is inconsistent with the notion of reasonableness. How could such a woman think "reasonably" if she is so debilitated by her abuse?

Though much is now understood about the physical and psychological brutalization experienced by battered women, much less is known about women as agents rather than victims of aggression. In learning more about the nature of women's aggression as well as their exercise of self-control, we may be in a better position to educate male jurists and offer advice to defense lawyers charged with presenting their cases to the court. *Reason* to a man means a detached appraisal of threat and the use of appropriate violence. *Reason* to a woman means holding to nonviolence until self-control finally snaps under too much exploitation. All reasonable women have a breaking point, and all reasonable women have a right to have that fact understood.

Madwomen and Badwomen

If the law seems perplexed and biased in its comprehension of aggression by women, so does the psychiatric establishment. Sometimes the two conspire to create situations of appalling inequity, as when criminal violence by women, so inexplicable to the male mind, and such a threat, is judged simultaneously bad *and* mad.

In England, alarming facts are being brought to light suggesting that women are doubly penalized for their aggression. After being found guilty of a criminal offense, particularly one involving elements of violence, women are far more likely to be labeled "mentally disordered."[21] Women comprise only 4 percent of the prison population but comprise 20 percent of the inmates sent for psychiatric treatment.[22] Being called mentally disordered is more than just a stigmatizing label that a woman must wear for the rest of her life. It opens the way for her to be transferred to "special hospitals," where she can be kept indefinitely—until such time as she has recovered from her illness.

These "hospitals" are designed to hold the most dangerous prisoners in the country, complete with high walls, barbed wire, and electronic doors. The "nurses" are members of the Prison Officers Association and wear prison-officer uniforms. In one special hospital, 66 percent of those in solitary confinement ("seclusion") were women, even though women made up only 30 percent of the inmates, and they clocked 80 percent of the total prisoner hours in confinement. Most are sent there because of acts of aggression directed at themselves. It should come as no surprise that, trained to view aggression against others as wrong, women would be especially likely to express their frustration and stress in self-injury. But in so doing they evidently prove that they are indeed crazy. Women in Special Hospitals, a movement aimed at remedying these injustices, offers this harrowing insight into the Kafkaesque nightmare through which these women live:

> In 1984, when S was eighteen, she was arrested and convicted of assault and sentenced to two years in prison. Most of her sentence was spent on the psychiatric unit. At that time, due to staff shortages women on the unit were frequently locked up for twenty-three hours out of twenty-four. Unable to read or write (a lifeline for many women in prison), S spent many hours alone in her cell. During this time she self-mutilated, damaged her cell, showed violence toward staff, and set fire to her bedding. Because of these incidents, she spent much of her time in "strips"—her furniture was removed from the cell (except a mattress, although that too could be taken out), and she was stripped of all clothing apart from a reinforced nylon shift. She had no underclothes or shoes. She could be in this condition for days. S was due to be released in the summer of 1986. In July 1985, at the request of the prison psychiatrist, she was assessed for admission to a special hospital but was found not to fulfill the criteria as laid down by the Mental Health Act at that time. Six months later, just six months before the date on which she was due to be released, she was assessed again. This time she was accepted and was diagnosed as suffering from a psychopathic disorder. She was admitted to a special hospital in February 1986—a few months before she was due to be released from prison. Three and a half years later she was still in prison.[23]

S's story is a vivid example of unexamined psychiatric labels that allow women to be held at the discretion of doctors long after serving their prison sentences. Deprived of hope and dignity, frustrated by a system they can barely understand, let alone fight, these women become anxious, depressed, and finally self-destructive. Women's aggression is not used as it is by male prisoners to intimidate, control, or coerce. It does not happen as a response to a perceived slight, a determination to get an extra ration of cigarettes, or to sexually exploit or humiliate. It is directed as often against the woman herself as against anyone else. It doesn't look anything like men's aggression. And that, apparently, is evidence of its insanity.

PMS: Hormones and Hysteria

The medical establishment has also played its part in translating less grievous forms of female aggression into simple, exclusively female issues. Premenstrual syndrome, or PMS, is increasingly invoked to explain outbursts of anger among women that occur sporadically and, to the male mind, with no apparent reason. Women who by all accounts should be content with their lives—often happily married and with children, from comfortable homes, with no criminal history—from time to time erupt in anger and frustration. These explosions seem unrelated to any acts of provocation and serve no obvious instrumental goals. They are "senseless" acts yet, because they are episodic rather than constant, they cannot be explained by an enduring personality disorder or a continuing mental disability.

Enter the villains of the piece: female hormones, with their cyclical variations and mysteriously wicked effects. These invisible agents can transform loving and obedient wives into hell-raising vixens. And what convenient rogues they are, since they banish from further consideration the possibility that all may not be well in the state of women's lives. We can now ignore the stresses imposed by the twenty-four-hour-a-day jobs of motherhood and domestic labor, as well as the grim facts of women's working lives, which slot them into low-paid, short-term, and part-time jobs or into the guilt-ridden choices that must often be made between mothering and employment. If the problem is not society or stress but simply hormones, then the cure lies not in drastic changes in the demands made upon women but in medication. As the British doctor Katherina Dalton explains in the introduction to *Once a Month*:

> Once a month with monotonous regularity, chaos is inflicted on over a million British homes as premenstrual tension and other menstrual problems recur time and time again with demoralizing repetition. This book explains how these menstrual problems can be completely relieved with the proper treatment, just as the pains of

childbirth are today universally treated with pain-relievers and anaesthetics.[24]

Before we all run to our doctors, we should be aware that the treatments that have been used include sterilization and hysterectomy, speculatively performed in the hope (as it turned out, unfounded) that they would cure premenstrual syndrome.[25] Today pharmaceuticals (drugs and synthetic hormones) are more often used instead: progesterone, progestogens, testosterone, bromocriptine, pyridoxine, lithium, and antidepressants. Their side effects include addiction, deepening of the voice, facial hair growth, masculinization of any female child conceived during treatment, restlessness, insomnia, and dysmenorrhea. The most widely used treatment, progesterone therapy, has received only two adequately designed clinical trials, both of which have reported negative results.[26]

PMS was first explained in 1931 by the psychiatrist Robert Frank as "indescribable tension," "irritability," and "a desire to find relief by foolish and ill-conceived actions."[27] Today it remains just as elusive, with over 150 different imputed symptoms.[28] The big three, however, are tiredness, depression, and irritability—with the last of these seen as the most significant and socially dangerous. It is called a *syndrome* rather than a disease because it is simply a collection of varied antisocial behaviors that cluster inexplicably together. Medical thought dictates that where several problems occur together, they are seen as symptoms of some *underlying disorder* rather than merely representing what they appear to be—in this case, a woman's dissatisfaction with her life. So PMS is the surface manifestation of a clinical condition that doctors believe to be caused by cyclical imbalances in the body.

No one knows why, as one husband put it, a "wonderful wife with her perfect figure and lovely nature spit[s] with rage for no obvious reason once a month."[29] Possibilities include decreased estrogen, changes in progesterone, effects on prolactin, endometrial toxins, nutritional deficiencies, glucose metabolism, vitamin B deficiency, and endorphin-level changes, to name but a few.[30] It is suggested that one or all of these changes affect brain neurotransmitters (possibly monoamino oxidase or catecholamine). At present these are no more than educated guesses. Indeed, the American Psychiatric

Association has so far listed PMS, which it calls "late luteal-phase dysphoric disorder," only in the appendix of its diagnostic manual, refusing to put it in the body of the text until systematic research confirms its existence.

How are we to know if we are the innocent sufferers of PMS or just spoiled hellcats? According to Dalton, the widely accepted expert in the field, the person most likely to make an accurate diagnosis is the long-suffering husband. It is he, not the woman, who is victim, diagnostician, doctor, and therapist:

> How many wives batter their husbands during the paramenstruum is unknown, or how often *the husband is provoked beyond reason and batters her*. . . . Not uncommonly the husbands have devised their own means of confirming the diagnosis beforehand; thus the computer magnate came complete with a computer printout to prove it, while a draughtsman turned up with a beautifully drawn blueprint; others merely bring along the office diary or kitchen calendar. But there are *too many husbands who have not made the diagnosis* or, more rarely, do not realize that help is available. They may know when they wake up that it's one of those days and no matter what they do, they will not be able to satisfy her. If he returns home with some red roses she'll ask "Why didn't you bring me my favorite chocolates?" but when he brings the correct brand of chocolates, it'll be "You know I'm dieting, how very cruel of you." He just can't win. . . . He will also find that he is the first to notice the warning signs of the premenstrual syndrome. The slight irrationality of her conversation, or lack of conversation, the minor *disagreements in which there is a certain rigidity to her views*. . . . If at this time the fiancé or husband suggests that she should start her treatment or go to the doctor, he will receive a flat denial that anything is wrong. In fact she is quite unaware of the changes taking place, but *this rigid refusal is another sure sign*. If she is already on progesterone therapy, *the husband can then insist* that she start using her progesterone suppositories.[31] [Emphasis added.]

Since the nature of the disorder, Dalton argues, renders women unstable, unable to recognize their own illness, it falls to the sane, objective man of the house to tell them what their problem is and to "insist" that they take their medication. (Woe betide the hapless single woman who lacks a live-in diagnostician.) If a woman resists his suggestion or continues to argue with him, she offers proof of the accuracy of his diagnosis.

Researchers have directed their attention to circumstantial evidence of the existence of PMS by charting the moods and actions of women at different points in the menstrual cycle. But this data is itself fraught with problems.[32] Some authors have taken as their "time at risk" of aggression the paramenstruum—this includes the week before the onset of menstruation as well as the time of menstruation itself. No rationale is given for doing this, and it makes no logical sense to include menstruation in a study explicitly designed to investigate premenstruation. The result is that nearly two out of every four weeks are included in the vulnerability period. Little wonder, then, that 46 percent of criminally convicted women wound up committing their crimes during a period of time that spans half their cycle.[33]

So determined are some researchers to find the PMS effect that they overlook evidence to the contrary. One study found a relation between arousal and cycle phase in only 12 out of 72 statistical tests.[34] Another reported that 14 out of 75 measures showed the predicted cyclical variation[35] and, yet another,[36] 13 out of 129. Other studies have found monthly-cycle effects even among nonmenstruating individuals such as prepubertal girls[37] and criminal men.[38] One ingenious study compared women at identical phases of their menstrual cycles (six to seven days before their next menstrual period), but one group of women had been told they were only midway through their cycle while the other group was correctly informed that they were in the premenstrual phase. Those who could not attribute their experiences to their hormones, sure enough, reported far fewer symptoms.[39]

For most women, mood changes during the menstrual cycle are no greater than those occurring as a result of other factors in their lives,[40] and normal women show little evidence of depression, hostility, and anxiety in the premenstrual days. At least part of the answer to the peculiarly elusive nature of PMS is the common finding that it is experienced by only a *minority* of women in the population.[41] A theory in terms of social representations gives us some clues as to who these women might be. An expressive understanding of aggression views angry outbursts as self-indulgent and harmful to others.

They induce strong feelings of guilt and anxiety. The more fearful a woman is of her inability to control her feelings and actions, the more guilt she will feel when she fails. When we do something that breaks ordinary social conventions, we all want to offer excuses for our behavior. Caught in a lie, we hurriedly explain that it was only to prevent someone's feelings from being hurt. When a child behaves like a monster in public, a parent is quick to point out that "he isn't usually like this." And when a woman, already concerned about her ability to repress her anger, actually snaps, she now finds a medically endorsed excuse: It is that time of the month.

The responsibility for the outburst is not hers but her hormones'. She splits her body off from her mind, as it were, and dumps all the guilt on the former. The availability of premenstrual syndrome as a widely held social representation makes this possible. Its "discovery" by science and its dissemination in the media have provided women with a means of disowning their anger. But those who are most likely to buy into such an explanation are those who have most reason to want to divorce themselves from antisocial feelings, lack of self-control, or the stresses and strains of daily life.

This anxiety about self-control is one of the defining features of neurosis. Neurosis is expressed in many forms, from a free-floating sense of tension to full-blown anxiety attacks embedded in phobias and compulsions. But what seems to be common to all these manifestations is a sense of dread about losing control over one's behavior—a sense that, at any minute, one might say or do something that betrays one as crazy. Not surprisingly, PMS is most often reported by psychiatrically disturbed populations.[42] And women who report premenstrual increases in irritability, tension, and anxiety also score highly on measures of neuroticism[43] and tend to experience anxiety and irritability at other times of the month, too.[44] Finally, women who report PMS are more likely to come from cultural and religious backgrounds, such as Judaism and Catholicism, that endorse traditional behavior and attitudes for women.[45]

It is too soon to say with any certainty whether PMS has any reliable neurochemical basis. And it is certainly not my intention to say that women who report it are crazy. There may be a minority of women for whom hormonal swings are sudden and intense enough to cause real changes in their emotional and physical well-being. But

I am convinced that their numbers are small, and in fact one government paper reported that only about 5 percent of women are seriously affected by premenstrual syndrome.[46] It is insulting to the other 95 percent to find their grievances and frustrations swept aside as hormonal upsets by doctors and husbands who want to ignore the possible real reasons for them. For those women with anxiety about experiencing unacceptable female behaviors like aggression who choose to hide behind the proffered mantle of "female problems," the help they need is not progesterone therapy, lithium, antidepressants, or hysterectomies. It is support that will allow them freely to say, "I'm angry," and not to fear the consequences of their words.

Gender and Power

One of the great benefits of power is the ability to define the "correct" interpretations of events. So natural and self-evident to men is their view of aggression as a form of coercion, control, and hence power that they cannot stand back and see it for what it is: one among many ways of interpreting violence. Among men, aggression is mundane and frequent. It demands a nonpathological account, for if every man who aggressed was deemed insane, there would be few sane men left.

But if I seem scathing of the male instrumental view of aggression, I am not convinced that the universal adoption of an expressive view is the answer. Women's orientation to aggression causes problems for them in large part because it is at odds with that of dominant male thought. But there are other difficulties, too. In tolerating frustration and provocation until a breaking point is reached, in making a virtue out of martyrdom, women as individuals and as a group risk losing their participation in the process of orderly and fair change. Whether within a marriage or within a society, it is only by speaking out that women can put their discontents and their solutions on the table.

Assertiveness training may help women in the short term to learn how to give voice to the well of emotions they feel *before* the point where tears and anger overwhelm them. But in the longer term, society must succeed in taking women seriously—beginning with their experiences in the first social institution they meet: the school.

Even in today's classrooms, girls speak less and are less often called upon than boys.[47] It is these early experiences that show women that their voices are not as legitimate as those of men and, in turn, that they should keep silent and tolerate opinions that differ from their own. The lesson is reinforced in the workplace, where women are effectively silent against the power and authority that continue to be vested in men. The personal distress that this causes women, and their higher rates of both neurosis and depression, are symptoms of the internal turmoil that comes with the daily stifling of one's anger.

A world where only an instrumental view of aggression existed would be a frightening place. War, robbery, terrorism, and bullying would be the property not only of men but of women too. But a wholly expressive world of aggression would be one in which the loudest sound would be the slow simmering of anger waiting to boil over. Perhaps a new representation needs to emerge—one that can be used and accepted by both sexes. We can only speculate about what that might be. Perhaps overt aggression will come to be seen as an embarrassing manifestation of our animal past. Perhaps people will blush, stammer, and apologize when they resort to that crudest and most primitive form of behavior.

That day seems a long way off. Between now and then, the sexes can at least begin to listen to one another. Women, raised in an androcentric world, already know much about male violence as a means of seizing control in the international arena, of securing sex and power in the crime of rape, and of developing masculinity in the swaggering adolescent group. But men have hardly begun to listen to women. The longer they shut out the voices of women, the more frustrated women are going to become at the manifest injustice they receive at men's hands. When women and men can truly hear one another, women's anger will no longer be redefined or ignored. And women should not need to reach a breaking point in order, finally, for their concerns to be understood.

NOTES

Chapter 1. Cultural Lessons in Aggression

1. R. Fox, "The Inherent Rules of Violence," in *Social Rules and Social Behavior,* ed. P. Collett (Oxford: Basil Blackwell, 1977).
2. Previous writers have distinguished between hostile and instrumental acts. The first denotes acts in which the aim is to injure the victim, the second to acts in which aggression is used to gain some nonaggressive goal. The distinction here is between acts, while my dichotomy refers to theories. The terms also refer to different implied goals than those suggested by my distinction between instrumental and expressive theories. (See A. H. Buss, *The Psychology of Aggression* [New York: Wiley, 1961]; idem, "Aggression Pays," in *The Control of Aggression and Violence: Cognitive and Physiological Factors,* ed. J. L. Singer [New York: Academic Press, 1971]; S. Feshbach, "The Function of Aggression and the Regulation of Aggressive Drive," *Psychological Review* 71 [1964]: 257–72; and idem, "Aggression," in *Carmichael's Manual of Child Psychology,* vol. 2, ed. P. H. Mussen [New York: Wiley, 1970].)
3. S. Freud, "Warum Krieg?" in *Gesammelte Werke,* vol. 16 (London: Imago, 1950). Useful reviews of Freud's position can be found in D. Zillmann, *Hostility and Aggression* (Hillsdale, N.J.: Erlbaum, 1979) and Buss, *Psychology of Aggression.*
4. M. A. Straus, R. J. Gelles, and S. Steinmetz, *Behind Closed Doors: Violence in the American Family* (New York: Anchor Press, 1980); M. A. Straus and R. J. Gelles, *Physical Violence in American Families: Risk Factors and*

Adaptations to Violence in 8,145 Families (New Brunswick, N.J.: Transaction, 1990).

5. J. Monahan, *Predicting Violent Behavior: An Assessment of Clinical Techniques* (Beverly Hills, Calif.: Sage, 1981).
6. J. E. Hokanson, "Psychophysiological Evaluation of the Catharsis Hypothesis," in *The Dynamics of Aggression: Individual, Group and International Analyses,* ed. E. I. Megargee and J. E. Hokanson (New York: Harper and Row, 1970).
7. J. Dollard, L. W. Doob, N. E. Miller, O. H. Mowrer, and R. R. Sears, *Frustration and Aggression* (New Haven, Conn.: Yale University Press, 1939).
8. N. E. Miller, "The Frustration-Aggression Hypothesis," *Psychological Review* 48 (1941): 337–42.
9. A. Aichhorn, *Wayward Youth* (New York: Meridian Books, 1955; orig. pub. 1925); F. Redl and H. Toch, "The Psychoanalytic Perspective," in *Psychology of Crime and Criminal Justice,* ed. H. Toch (Prospect Heights, Ill.: Waveland, 1986), pp. 183–97; F. Perls, *In and Out of the Garbage Pail* (Lafayette, Calif.: Real People Press, 1969).
10. M. Gottfredson and T. Hirschi, *A General Theory of Crime* (Stanford, Calif.: Stanford University Press, 1990); T. Hirschi, *Causes of Delinquency* (Berkeley: University of California Press, 1969).
11. O. H. Mowrer and R. Lamoreaux, "Fear as an Intervening Variable in Avoidance Conditioning," *Journal of Comparative and Physiological Psychology* 39 (1946): 29–50; H. J. Eysenck, *Crime and Personality* (London: Routledge and Kegan Paul, 1964).
12. G. R. Patterson, "The Aggressive Child: Victim and Architect of a Coercive System," in *Behavior Modification and Families,* ed. L. A. Hamerlynch, L. C. Handy, and E. J. Mash, vol. 1: *Theory and Research* (New York: Brunner/Mazell, 1976); A. Bandura, *Aggression: A Social Learning Analysis* (Engelwood Cliffs, N.J.: Prentice-Hall, 1973).
13. H. Toch, *Violent Men: An Inquiry into the Psychology of Violence* (Chicago: Aldine, 1969).
14. M. Wolfgang and F. Ferracuti, *The Subculture of Violence* (New York: Barnes and Noble, 1967); T. J. Bernard, "Angry Aggression Among the Truly Disadvantaged," *Criminology* 28 (1990): 73–95.
15. A. Campbell, "The Streets and Violence," in *Violent Transactions: The Limits of Personality,* ed. A. Campbell and J. Gibbs (Boston: Basil Blackwell, 1986).
16. J. T. Tedeschi, R. B. Smith, and R. C. Brown, "A Reinterpretation of Research on Aggression," *Psychological Bulletin* 81 (1974): 540–62.

17. T. Schelling (1966), cited in ibid., p. 550.
18. D. Black, "Crime as Social Control," *American Sociological Review* 48, no. 1 (1983): 34–35.
19. B. Spock and M. B. Rothenberg, *Dr. Spock's Baby and Child Care* (New York: Pocket Books, 1985), p. 384.
20. P. Leach, *Your Baby and Child: From Birth to Age Five* (New York: Knopf, 1987), p. 440.
21. S. Moscovici, *La psychanalyse: Son image et son public* (Paris: Presses Universitaires de France, 1976).
22. S. Moscovici, "On Social Representations," in *Social Cognition: Perspectives on Everyday Understanding,* ed. J. Forgas (London: Academic Press, 1981); idem, "The Phenomenon of Social Representations," in *Social Representations,* ed. R. Farr and S. Moscovici (Cambridge: Cambridge University Press, 1984).
23. J. Piaget, *Judgment and Reasoning in the Child* (New York: Harcourt Brace, 1926).
24. This discussion relies heavily upon N. Emler, "Socio-moral Development from the Perspective of Social Representations," *Journal for the Theory of Social Behavior* 17 (1987): 371–88, and M. Hewstone and S. Moscovici, "Social Representations and Social Explanations: From the 'Naive' to the 'Amateur' Scientist," in *Attribution Theory,* ed. M. Hewstone (Oxford: Basil Blackwell, 1982), pp. 48–125.
25. R. Farr, "Social Representations: A French Tradition of Research," *Journal for the Theory of Social Behavior* 17 (1987): 343–70; R. M. Farr and S. Moscovici, *Social Representations* (New York: Cambridge University Press, 1984).

Chapter 2. Boys, Girls, and Aggression

1. B. I. Fagot, M. D. Leinbach, and R. Hagan, "Gender Labeling and the Development of Sex-Typed Behaviors," *Developmental Psychology* 22, no. 4 (1986): 440–43; F. Goodenough, *Anger in Young Children* (Minneapolis: University of Minnesota Press, 1931).
2. G. R. Patterson, "Multiple Evaluations of a Parent Training Program," in *Applications of Behavior Modification,* ed. T. Thompson and W. S. Dockens (New York: Academic Press, 1975); A. Bandura, *Aggression: A Social Learning Analysis* (Englewood Cliffs, N.J.: Prentice-Hall, 1975); W. Mischel, "A Social-Learning View of Sex Differences in Behavior," in *The Development of Sex Differences,* ed. E. E. Maccoby (Stanford: Stanford University Press, 1966).

3. E. Maccoby, *Social Development: Psychological Growth and the Parent-Child Relationship* (New York: Harcourt Brace Jovanovich, 1980).
4. E. E. Maccoby and C. N. Jacklin, *The Psychology of Sex Differences* (Stanford: Stanford University Press, 1974); idem, "Sex Differences in Aggression: A Rejoinder and Reprise," *Child Development* 51 (1980): 964–80; T. Tieger, "On the Biological Basis of Sex Differences in Aggression," *Child Development* 51 (1980): 943–63.
5. Goodenough, *Anger in Young Children.*
6. J. Langlois and A. Downes, "Mothers and Peers as Socialization Agents of Sex-Typed Play Behaviors in Young Children," Psychology Dept., University of Texas, Austin, 1979.
7. M. E. Snow, C. N. Jacklin, and E. E. Maccoby, "Sex of Child Differences in Father-Child Interaction at One Year," *Child Development* 54 (1983): 227–32.
8. P. Leach, *Your Baby and Child: From Birth to Age Five* (New York: Knopf, 1987).
9. N. Frude, "The Physical Abuse of Children," in *Clinical Approaches to Aggression and Violence,* ed. K. Howells and C. Hollin (Leicester, U.K.: British Psychological Society, 1988).
10. L. Kohlberg, "A Cognitive-Developmental Analysis of Children's Sex-Role Concepts and Attitudes," in Maccoby, *Development of Sex Differences.*
11. P. A. Katz, "Gender Identity: Development and Consequences," in *The Social Psychology of Female-Male Relations: A Critical Analysis of Central Concepts,* ed. R. Ashmore and F. Del Boco (New York: Academic Press, 1986), pp. 21–68.
12. J. Money, J. G. Hampson, and J. L. Hampson, "Imprinting and the Establishment of Gender Role," *American Medical Association Archives of Neurology and Psychiatry* 77 (1957): 333–36.
13. Katz, "Gender Identity"; D. G. Perry and K. Bussey, "The Social Learning Theory of Sex Differences: Imitation Is Alive and Well," *Journal of Personality and Social Psychology* 37 (1979): 1699–1712; C. L. Martin and C. F. Halverson, "A Schematic Processing Model of Sex Typing and Stereotyping in Children," *Child Development* 52 (1981): 1119–34; B. I. Fagot, "Beyond the Reinforcement Principle: Another Step Toward an Understanding of Sex Role Development," *Developmental Psychology* 21, no. 6 (1985): 1097–1104.
14. Kohlberg, "Cognitive-Developmental Analysis."
15. Fagot, Leinbach, and Hagan, "Gender Labeling."

16. This analysis follows N. Chodorow, *The Reproduction of Mothering* (Berkeley: University of California Press, 1978).
17. J. Hagan, J. Simpson, and A. R. Gillis, "Feminist Scholarship, Relational and Instrumental Control, and a Power-Control Theory of Gender and Delinquency," *British Journal of Sociology* 39 (1988): 301–36; quotation is on p. 320.
18. W. Damon, *The Social World of the Child* (San Francisco: Jossey-Bass, 1977), p. 255.
19. E. Goodenough, "Interest in Persons as an Aspect of Sex Differences in the Early Years," *Genetic Psychology Monographs* 55 (1957): 287–323; quotation is on p. 310.
20. J. Archer, "Childhood Gender Roles: Social Context and Organization," in *Childhood Social Development: Contemporary Perspectives,* ed. H. McGurk (Hillsdale, N.J.: Erlbaum, 1992).
21. R. G. Slaby and F. S. Frey, "Development of Gender Constancy and Selective Attention to Same-Sex Models," *Child Development* 46 (1975): 849–56; K. Durkin, "Children's Accounts of Sex Role Stereotypes in Television," *Communications Research* 11 (1984): 341–62.
22. Kohlberg, "Cognitive-Developmental Analysis."
23. E. Maccoby, "Gender as Social Category," *Developmental Psychology* 24 (1988): 755–65; E. Maccoby and C. Jacklin, "Gender Segregation in Childhood," in *Advances in Childhood Development and Behavior,* ed. H. W. Reese, vol. 20 (New York: Academic Press, 1987), pp. 239–87.
24. Fagot, "Beyond the Reinforcement Principle," p. 1102.
25. B. I. Fagot and R. Hagan, "Aggression in Toddlers: Responses to the Assertive Acts of Boys and Girls," *Sex Roles* 12 (1985): 341–51; B. I. Fagot, R. Hagan, H. D. Leinbach, and S. Kronsberg, "Differential Reactions to Assertive and Communicative Acts of Toddler Boys and Girls," *Child Development* 56 (1985): 1499–1505.
26. B. Lloyd and C. Smith, "The Effects of Age and Gender on Social Behavior in Very Young Children," *British Journal of Social Psychology* 25 (1986): 219–30; G. Duveen and B. Lloyd, "The Significance of Social Identities," *British Journal of Social Psychology* 25 (1986): 219–30; Fagot and Hagan, "Aggression in Toddlers."
27. F. F. Strayer and J. Strayer, "An Ethological Analysis of Social Agonism and Dominance Relations Among Preschool Children," *Child Development* 47 (1976): 980–89; W. C. McGrew, *An Ethological Analysis of Children's Behavior* (New York: Academic Press, 1972).

28. W. H. Hartup, "Aggression in Childhood: Developmental Perspectives," *American Psychologist* 29 (1974): 336–41.
29. J. Archer, "Gender Roles as Developmental Pathways," *British Journal of Social Psychology* 23 (1984): 245–56; D. S. David and R. Brannon, "The Male Sex Role: Our Culture's Blueprint of Manhood and What It's Done for Us Lately," in *The Forty-Nine Percent Majority: The Male Sex Role,* ed. D. S. David and R. Brannon (Reading, Mass.: Addison-Wesley, 1976); R. E. Hartley, "Sex-Role Pressures and the Socialization of the Male Child," *Psychological Reports* 5 (1959): 457–68.
30. Fagot, "Beyond the Reinforcement Principle."
31. J. S. Hyde, B. G. Rosenberg, and J. A. Behrman, "Tomboyism," *Psychology of Women Quarterly* 2 (1977): 73–75.
32. Archer, "Childhood Gender Roles."
33. P. Giordano, S. A. Cernkovich, and M. D. Pugh, "Friendships and Delinquency," *American Journal of Sociology* 91, no. 5 (1986): 1170–1202; H. C. Foot, A. J. Chapman, and J. R. Smith, *Friendship and Social Relations in Childhood* (Chichester, U.K.: Wiley, 1980); Archer, "Childhood Gender Roles"; Maccoby and Jacklin, "Gender Segregation in Childhood"; M. Waldrop and C. Halverson, "Intensive and Extensive Peer Behavior: Longitudinal and Cross-Sectional Analysis," *Child Development* 46 (1975): 19–26.
34. Fagot, Leinbach, and Hagan, "Gender Labeling."
35. Fagot et al., "Differential Reactions."

3. Fighting Aggression: Women and Anger

1. A. Campbell and S. Muncer, "Models of Anger and Aggression in the Social Talk of Women and Men," *Journal for the Theory of Social Behavior* 17 (1987): 489–512; A. Campbell, S. Muncer, and E. Coyle, "Social Representations of Aggression as an Explanation of Gender Differences: A Preliminary Study," *Aggressive Behavior* 18 (1992): 95–108; A. Campbell, S. Muncer, and B. Gorman, "Gender and Social Representations of Aggression: A Communal-Agentic Analysis," *Aggressive Behavior* (forthcoming).
2. M. Straus, R. Gelles, and S. Steinmetz, *Behind Closed Doors: Violence in the American Family* (New York: Anchor Press/Doubleday, 1980).
3. D. Tannen, *You Just Don't Understand: Women and Men in Conversation* (New York: Morrow, 1990).

4. D. Maltz and R. Borker, "A Cultural Approach to Male-Female Miscommunication," in *Language and Social Identity,* ed. J. Gumperz (New York: Cambridge University Press, 1982), pp. 196–216.
5. H. Lerner, *The Dance of Anger: A Woman's Guide to Changing the Pattern of Intimate Relationships* (New York: Harper and Row, 1985).

4. Fair Game and Fair Fights: Aggression Among Men

1. R. Felson, "Aggression as Impression Management," *Social Psychology Quarterly* 41 (1978): 215–31; R. Felson, "Impression Management and the Escalation of Aggression and Violence," *Social Psychology Quarterly* 45 (1982): 245–54; L. Athens, *Violent Criminal Acts and Actors: A Symbolic Interactionist Study* (Boston: Routledge and Kegan Paul, 1980); D. Luckenbill, "Criminal Homicide as a Situated Transaction," *Social Problems* 25 (1977): 176–86.
2. J. Katz, *Seductions of Crime: Moral and Sensual Attractions of Doing Evil* (New York: Basic Books, 1988).
3. H. Toch, *Violent Men* (Chicago: Aldine, 1969).
4. D. Tannen, *You Just Don't Understand: Women and Men in Conversation* (New York: Morrow, 1990).
5. In this regard, male fighting sounds much like the kind of ritual confrontation described vividly by ethologists. In man, however, as in other mammals, threat alone rarely suffices. Some kind of limited attack often follows. To the extent that the people or animals involved do not possess lethal capabilities, little serious damage is likely. The real danger lies in the possibility of firearms. These would be outlawed in the traditional fair fight. Sadly, this seems to be becoming an outmoded rule among young, urban males. (See R. Hinde, *Animal Behavior: A Synthesis of Ethology and Comparative Psychology,* 2d ed. [New York: McGraw-Hill, 1970]; I. Eibl-Eibesfeldt, *Love and Hate: The Natural History of Behavior Patterns* [New York: Holt, Rinehart and Winston, 1971].)
6. M. Straus, R. Gelles, and S. Steinmetz, *Behind Closed Doors: Violence in the American Family* (New York: Anchor Press/Doubleday, 1980).
7. A. Ganley, *Participants' Manual: Court-Mandated Therapy for Men Who Batter: A Three-Day Workshop for Professionals* (Washington, D.C.: Center for Women's Policy Studies, 1981); E. Stark and J. McEvoy, "Middle Class Violence," *Psychology Today* 4, no. 6 (1970): 107–12.

5. Gender and the Shape of Aggression

1. In these experiments men and women are brought into psychology labs and allowed to express aggression. The classic version of this kind of design is one in which the subjects believe they are taking the role of teacher in a learning experiment. Each time another subject makes an error on a learning task, the "teachers" are told to deliver electric shocks, at a voltage they may choose, to the hapless student (actually a stooge of the experimenter, who is not in fact receiving any shocks).

   Other studies provide the subject with the opportunity to write negative evaluations of the stooge, which will (so the innocent subjects believe) have an effect on that person's grades or job. Some ingenious researchers move from the laboratory out into the real world, sending stooges to cut into lines at supermarket checkouts or to stall their cars at traffic lights. They then observe the behavior of the men and women who are inconvenienced by the apparent rudeness or incompetence. Using these basic designs, psychologists can study the effects of a number of variables on gender differences in aggression. They can see whether insulting or provoking the subjects changes the size of sex differences in willingness to aggress. They can place observers in the situation to see whether men and women react differently when they are being watched. They can, in short, try to isolate those factors that increase or decrease the size of sex differences in aggression. Hundreds of studies of this kind have been done.

   In recent years a new statistical technique called *meta-analysis* has become available that has helped researchers to find their way through this maze of psychological studies. Simultaneously considering dozens of experiments, it produces a statement of the magnitude of the sex differences across all of them. The overall size of the gender difference is given by a statistic called *d*. No difference between the sexes gives a *d* of zero. A *d* of .50 or more is large enough for the average person to notice. Adult men in the kinds of laboratory studies just discussed are more aggressive than women (d = .29), and little boys, observed largely in natural settings like playgrounds, are much more aggressive than little girls (d = .50).

   So meta-analysis can confirm our impression that there are gender differences in aggression, but it can also tell us about the factors that increase or decrease the size of the difference. The difference between .29 and .50, for example, seems to suggest that either age or the experimental situation decreases sex differences. It turns out that both of these factors has an effect. If we look only at children, but split the studies according to whether the data came from an experiment or from natural observation, the *d* moves from .56 for naturalistic studies to .29 for experiments. At the same time, if we pool different types of study but split by age, we find that children under six have a *d* of .58, which by college age has decreased to .27. Meta-analysis takes social science into a more sophisticated realm. The problem is no longer explaining why men are more aggressive but explaining why this aggression difference ebbs and flows with differing circumstances. (See G. V. Glass, B. McGaw, and M. L. Smith, *Meta-analysis in Social Research* [Beverly Hills, Calif.: Sage, 1981]; J. S. Hyde and M. C. Linn, *The Psychology of Gender: Advances Through Meta-analysis* [Baltimore: Johns Hopkins University Press, 1986].)

2. For psychologists, a *trait* is a tendency to respond in a consistent manner across different situations and across time. A term like *extrovert* is of real use only if it accurately describes a person's behavior over different settings and over a period of at least months, preferably years, of their lives. In the early 1970s, trait psychology underwent a crisis when it was documented that people in fact show a great deal of variability in their reactions. A person who is extroverted at a party may be painfully shy at a board meeting. And someone who is an extrovert today may show up in the same situation as an introvert next month. Trait psychologists were forced to acknowledge the guiding influence of cognition on action. Nevertheless, personality researchers maintained that consistency could be found in the long haul when behavior was averaged over dozens of settings and over not too large a time span. (Men are found to be more consistent in their aggression, whether high or low, than women—as we would expect, since women's tendency to explode depends upon the degree of stress they are under and is therefore more situationally variable than is men's. Also, men who find that aggression works would tend to use it consistently and at a high rate, and men who cannot use it effectively would show an equally consistent low rate of use.) (See W. Mischel, *Personality and Assessment* [New York: Wiley, 1968]; A. Campbell and J. Gibbs, *Violent Transactions: The Limits of Personality* [Oxford and Cambridge, Mass.: Basil Blackwell, 1986].)
3. C. Tavris, *Anger: The Misunderstood Emotion,* 2d ed. (New York: Touchstone, 1989); J. S. Hyde, "Gender Differences in Aggression," in *The*

Psychology of Gender, ed. Hyde and Linn; A. Frodi, J. Macauley, and P. R. Thome, "Are Women Always Less Aggressive Than Men? A Review of the Experimental Literature," *Psychological Bulletin* 84 (1977): 634–60.

4. D. Fitz, "Anger Expression by Women and Men in Five Natural Locations," paper presented to the American Psychological Association, New York, September 1979; D. Fitz, "The Social Ecology of Anger: A Profile of a Metropolitan Population," paper presented to the Symposium on Violence and the Violent Individual, Houston, Texas, November 1978; W. D. Frost and J. R. Averill, "Differences Between Men and Women in the Everyday Experience of Anger," in *Anger and Aggression: An Essay on Emotion,* ed. J. R. Averill (New York: Springer-Verlag, 1982).
5. Allen and Haccoun (1976), reported in Frost and Averill, "Differences Between Men and Women."
6. See Frost and Averill, "Differences Between Men and Women."
7. Ibid., p. 295.
8. See Frodi, Macauley, and Thome, "Are Women Always Less Aggressive?" The connection between anger and aggression has also been examined by meta-analysis. Alice Eagly and Valerie Steffen analyzed seventy-seven studies that used varying attempts to make the subject angry. They distinguished between slight provocation (some impediment to the subject's progress) and more than minimal provocation (such as insults, physical harm, and violation of rights) and found that the degree of provocation showed no relation to the magnitude of sex differences. Men were more aggressive than women regardless of the level of anger that the experiment had generated in them. Once again, this suggests that it is not men's greater anger that makes them more violent. ("Gender and Aggressive Behavior: A Meta-analytic Review of the Social Psychological Literature," *Psychological Bulletin* 100 [1986]: 309–30.)
9. "You Could Almost Smell the Fear. It Made Me Powerful," *The Independent,* London, May 16, 1991.
10. See D. F. Halpern, *Sex Differences in Cognitive Abilities* (Hillsdale, N.J.: Erlbaum, 1986).
11. The suggestion that women substituted words for blows was put to the test in two meta-analytic studies. The first included thirty-one studies with subjects ranging in age from toddlers to college age and found a much larger effect size (d = .60) for physical than for verbal (d = .43) aggression. A second study used fifty studies of adults college-aged or

older and similarly found larger gender differences on physical (d = .40) than on psychological aggression (d = .18). Men exceed women in both forms of aggression, though the effect is more marked in physical aggression. (See Hyde, "Gender Differences in Aggression," and Eagly and Steffen, "Gender and Aggressive Behavior.")

12. R. B. Felson and H. S. Steadman, "Situations and Processes Leading to Criminal Violence," *Criminology* 21 (1983): 59–74; R. B. Felson, "Patterns of Aggressive Social Interaction," in *Social Psychology of Aggression,* ed. A. Mummendey (New York: Springer-Verlag, 1984); J. Hepburn, "Violent Behavior in Interpersonal Relationships," *Sociological Quarterly* 14 (1973): 176–86; D. Luckenbill, "Criminal Homicide as a Situated Transaction," *Social Problems* 25 (1977): 176–86.
13. M. Straus and R. Gelles, "Societal Change and Change in Family Violence from 1975 to 1985 as Revealed by Two National Surveys," *Journal of Marriage and the Family* 48 (1986): 465–79; M. Straus, R. Gelles, and S. Steinmetz, *Behind Closed Doors: Violence in the American Family* (New York: Anchor Books/Doubleday, 1981).
14. Straus, Gelles, and Steinmetz, *Behind Closed Doors.*
15. K. E. MacEwan and J. Barling, "Multiple Stressors, Violence in the Family of Origin and Marital Aggression: A Longitudinal Investigation," *Journal of Family Violence* 3, no. 1 (1988): 73–87; J. E. Stets and M. A. Straus, "Gender Differences in Reporting Marital Violence and Its Medical and Psychological Consequences," in *Physical Violence in American Families: Risk Factors and Adaptations to Violence in 8,145 Families,* ed. M. Straus and R. Gelles (New Brunswick, N.J.: Transaction, 1990).
16. Straus and Gelles, *Physical Violence in American Families.*
17. D. Morris, *Babywatching* (London: Jonathan Cape, 1991).
18. B. Bach and P. Wyden, *The Intimate Enemy: How to Fight Fair in Love and Marriage* (New York: Avon Books, 1976).
19. See Frost and Averill, "Differences Between Men and Women."
20. B. Fagot, "Beyond the Reinforcement Principle: Another Step Toward an Understanding of Sex Role Development," *Developmental Psychology* 21 (1985): 1097–1104; B. Fagot and R. Hagan, "Assertion in Toddlers: Responses to Assertive Acts of Boys and Girls," *Sex Roles* 12 (1985): 341–51.
21. D. Tannen, *You Just Don't Understand* (New York: Morrow, 1990).
22. J. Archer, "Childhood Gender Roles: Social Context and Organization," in *Childhood Social Development: Contemporary Perspectives,* ed. H. McGurk (Hillsdale, N.J., and London: Erlbaum, 1991); E. E. Maccoby and C. N. Jacklin, "Gender Segregation in Childhood," in *Advances in*

Child Development and Behavior, ed. H. W. Reese, vol. 20 (New York: Academic Press, 1987).

23. See Eagly and Steffen, "Gender and Aggressive Behavior"; Frodi, Macauley, and Thome, "Are Women Always Less Aggressive?"
24. See Fitz, "Anger Expression by Women and Men."
25. A. Eagly, *Sex Differences in Social Behavior: A Social Role Interpretation* (Hillsdale, N.J.: Erlbaum, 1987).
26. See Fitz, "Anger Expression by Women and Men."
27. R. J. Borden, "Witnessed Aggression: Influence of an Observer's Sex and Values on Aggressive Responding," *Journal of Personality and Social Psychology* 31 (1975): 567–73.
28. M. C. Dertke, L. A. Penner, H. L. Hawkins, and C. Suarez, "The Inhibitory Effects of an Observer on Instrumental Aggression," *Bulletin of the Psychonomic Society* 1 (1973): 112–14.
29. Frodi, Macauley, and Thome, "Are Women Always Less Aggressive?"; Eagly and Steffen, "Gender and Aggressive Behavior"; Frost and Averill, "Differences Between Men and Women"; Eagly, *Sex Differences in Social Behavior.*
30. K. C. Smith, S. E. Ulch, J. E. Cameron, J. A. Cumberland, M. A. Musgrave, and N. Tremblay, "Gender-Related Effects in the Perception of Anger Expression," *Sex Roles* 20 (1989): 487–95; Frost and Averill, "Differences Between Men and Women"; Eagly, *Sex Differences in Social Behavior.*
31. R. R. Sears, "Relation of Early Socialization Experience to Aggression in Middle Childhood," *Journal of Abnormal and Social Psychology* 63 (1961): 466–92; D. M. Brodzinsky, S. M. Messer, and J. D. Tew, "Sex Differences in Children's Expression and Control of Fantasy and Overt Aggression," *Child Development* 50 (1979): 372–79; see also Frodi, Macauley, and Thome, "Are Women Always Less Aggressive?"
32. J. Kagan and H. A. Moss, *Birth to Maturity: A Study in Psychological Development* (New York: Wiley, 1962); I. M. Rosenstock, "Perceptual Aspects of Repression," *Journal of Abnormal and Social Psychology* 46 (1951): 304–15; M. Zuckerman, "The Effect of Frustration on the Perception of Neutral and Aggressive Words," *Journal of Personality* 23 (1955): 407–22; see Frodi, Macauley, and Thome, "Are Women Always Less Aggressive?"
33. Kagan and Moss, *Birth to Maturity;* T. R. Schill and L. Schneider, "Guilt and Self-Report of Hostility" and "Relationships Between Hostility Guilt and Several Measures of Hostility," *Psychological Reports* 27 (1970): 713–14; 967–70.

34. A. H. Buss and T. C. Brock, "Repression and Guilt in Relation to Aggression," *Journal of Abnormal and Social Psychology* 66 (1963): 345–50; T. C. Brock and A. H. Buss, "Effects of Justification for Aggression and Communication with the Victim on Postaggression Dissonance," *Journal of Abnormal and Social Psychology* 68 (1964): 403–12.
35. E. I. Rawlings, "Reactive Guilt and Anticipatory Guilt in Altruistic Behavior," in *Altruism and Helping Behavior*, ed. J. Macauley and L. Berkowitz (New York: Academic Press, 1970).
36. See Eagly and Steffen, "Gender and Aggressive Behavior."
37. J. B. Miller, *Toward a New Psychology of Women*, 2d ed. (Boston: Beacon, 1986); N. Chodorow, *The Reproduction of Mothering* (Berkeley: University of California Press, 1978).
38. J. T. Spence and R. L. Helmreich, *Masculinity and Femininity: Their Psychological Dimensions, Correlates and Antecedents* (Austin: University of Texas Press, 1978); S. L. Bem, "The Measurement of Psychological Androgyny," *Journal of Consulting and Clinical Psychology* 42 (1974): 155–62.
39. N. D. Feshbach and S. Feshbach, "Empathy Training and the Regulation of Aggression: Potentialities and Limitations," *Academic Psychology Bulletin* 4 (1982): 399–413.
40. G. Al-Issa, *Gender and Psychopathology* (London: Academic Press, 1982); C. S. Widom, "Toward an Understanding of Female Criminality," *Progress in Experimental Personality Research* 8 (1978): 245–308; R. D. Hare and D. Schalling, *Psychopathic Behavior: Approaches to Research* (Chichester, U.K.: Wiley, 1978).
41. H. Toch, *Violent Men* (Chicago: Aldine, 1969).
42. See Miller, *Toward a New Psychology.*
43. See Frost and Averill, "Differences Between Men and Women."
44. P. A. Miller and N. Eisenberg, "The Relation of Empathy to Aggressive and Externalizing/Antisocial Behavior," *Psychological Bulletin* 103 (1988): 324–44; see Eagly and Steffen, "Gender and Aggressive Behavior."
45. R. Y. Shapiro and H. Mahajan, "Gender Differences in Policy Preferences: A Summary of Trends from the 1960s to the 1980s," *Public Opinion Quarterly* 50 (1986): 42–61.
46. T. W. Smith, "The Polls: Gender and Attitudes Toward Violence," *Public Opinion Quarterly* 48 (1984): 384–96.
47. Ibid.
48. Ibid.
49. Ibid.

Chapter 6. Robbery

1. These and other U.S. criminal justice statistics on robbery in this chapter are taken from the United States Department of Justice, *Uniform Crime Reports* (Washington, D.C.: U.S. Government Printing Office, 1989).
2. If we examine self-report studies in which men and women tell researchers the offenses they have committed, the imbalance drops slightly, to around 6:1, from an official estimate of 13:1. Even so, startlingly few robberies are committed by women or even by groups that include only women. (M. Hindelang, T. Hirschi, and J. Weis, "Correlates of Delinquency," *American Sociological Review* 44 [1979]: 995–1014.)
3. One study found that only 1.8 percent of robbers mentioned losing their temper as the main motivation for the offense. (See S. Nugent, D. Burns, P. Wilson, and D. Chappell, *Risks and Rewards in Robbery: Prevention and the Offender's Perspective* [Sydney: Australian Institute for Criminology, 1989].) Several of the studies reported in this chapter specifically asked robbers about motive, victim choice, and state of mind at the time of the offense. None of the researchers mentions anger as relevant to any of these considerations.
4. D. Zillmann, *Hostility and Aggression* (Hillsdale, N.J.: Erlbaum, 1979), p. 194.
5. A. H. Buss, "Aggression Pays," in *The Control of Aggression and Violence: Cognitive and Physiological Factors*, ed. J. L. Singer (New York: Academic Press, 1971).
6. D. Walsh, *Heavy Business: Commercial Burglary and Robbery* (London and Boston: Routledge and Kegan Paul, 1986), p. 60.
7. J. Katz, *Seductions of Crime: The Moral and Sensual Attractions of Doing Evil* (New York: Basic Books, 1988), p. 244.
8. E. Fortune, M. Vega, and I. J. Silverman, "A Study of Female Robbers in a Southern Correctional Institution," *Journal of Criminal Justice* 8 (1980): 317–25; see also D. Girouard, "Les femmes incarcérées pour vol qualifié à Quebec, en 1985: Importance de leur role," *Canadian Journal of Criminology* (April 1988): 121–34.
9. Even this may be the result of the police coming down harder on men, so that they are more often arrested and prosecuted. Studies using self-report measures find that about twice as many men as women admit attacking someone with fists. (See Hindelang, Hirschi, and Weis, "Correlates of Delinquency.")

10. M. Straus and R. Gelles, *Physical Violence in American Families: Risk Factors and Adaptations to Violence in 8,145 Families* (New Brunswick, N.J.: Transaction, 1990); J. Archer and N. Ray, "Dating Violence in the United Kingdom: A Preliminary Study," *Aggressive Behavior* 15 (1989): 337–43; J. Makepeace, "Courtship Violence Among College Students," *Family Relations* 30 (1981): 97–102.
11. See P. J. Cook, "The Relationship Between Victim Resistance and Injury in Noncommercial Robbery," *Journal of Legal Studies* 15 (1986): 405–16; F. E. Zimring, "Determinants of the Death Rate from Robbery: A Detroit Time Study," *Journal of Legal Studies* 6 (1977): 317–32; F. E. Zimring and J. Zuehl, "Victim Injury and Death in Urban Robbery: A Chicago Study," *Journal of Legal Studies* 15 (1986): 1–40.
12. Girouard, "Les femmes incarcérées"; see also Fortune, Vega, and Silverman, "A Study of Female Robbers."
13. Bureau of Justice Statistics, *Criminal Victimization in the United States, 1987* (Washington, D.C.: U.S. Government Printing Office, 1989).
14. C. W. Harlow, *Special Report: Robbery Victims* (Washington, D.C.: U.S. Government Printing Office, 1987).
15. In fact, the amount of money taken in robbery is relatively small, considering the risks. In the United States, the average noncommercial robbery take is about $80. (T. Gabor, M. Baril, M. Cusson, D. Eli, M. Leblanc, and A. Normandeau, *Armed Robbery: Cops, Robbers and Victims* [Springfield, Ill.: Charles C Thomas, 1987]; J. Allen, *Assault with a Deadly Weapon: The Autobiography of a Street Criminal* [New York: McGraw-Hill, 1978]; Walsh, *Heavy Business.*)
16. Gabor et al., *Armed Robbery*, p. 63.
17. S. McLanahan, A. Sorensen, and D. Watson, "Sex Differences in Poverty, 1950–1980," *Signs* 15, no. 1 (1989): 162–222.
18. *The Independent*, London, April 23, 1991.
19. D. J. Steffensmeier and M. Cobb, "Sex Differences in Urban Arrest Patterns, 1934–79," *Social Problems* 29 (1981): 37–50; quotation is on p. 43.
20. Walsh, *Heavy Business.*
21. Katz, *Seductions of Crime.*
22. Allen, *Assault with a Deadly Weapon*, pp. 43, 103.
23. S. Schachter, "The Interaction of Cognitive and Physiological Determinants of Emotional State," in *Advances in Experimental Social Psychology*, ed. L. Berkowitz, vol. 1 (New York: Academic Press, 1964).
24. Harlow, *Special Report.*
25. D. F. Luckenbill, "Patterns of Force in Robbery," *Deviant Behavior* 1

(1980): 361–78; idem, "Generating Compliance: The Case of Robbery," *Urban Life* 10 (1981): 25–46.

26. J. Irwin, *The Felon* (Englewood Cliffs, N.J.: Prentice-Hall, 1970).
27. R. Lejeune, "The Management of a Mugging," *Urban Life* 6, no. 2 (1977): 123–48; quotation on p. 135.
28. Gabor et al., *Armed Robbery,* p. 58.
29. Harlow, *Special Report.*
30. Katz, *Seductions of Crime,* p. 190.
31. Gabor et al., *Armed Robbery;* Walsh, *Heavy Business.*
32. Lejeune, "Management of a Mugging," p. 134.
33. Katz, *Seductions of Crime.*
34. E. Miller, *Street Woman* (Philadelphia: Temple University Press, 1986); S. Cunningham, "Aspects of Violence in Prostitution," in *Perspectives on Rape and Sexual Assault,* ed. J. Hopkins (New York: Harper and Row, 1984).
35. H. Williamson, *Hustler! The Autobiography of a Thief* (New York: Doubleday, 1965); J. Carr, *Bad* (New York: Evans, 1975); B. Jackson, *Outside the Law: A Thief's Primer* (New Brunswick, N.J.: Transaction, 1972); J. Willwerth, *Jones* (New York: Evans, 1974); E. Anderson, *A Place on the Corner* (Chicago: Chicago University Press, 1978); M. Hannerz, *Soulside* (New York: Columbia University Press, 1969); E. Liebow, *Tally's Corner* (Boston: Little, Brown, 1967); A. Campbell, "The Streets and Violence," in *Violent Transactions: The Limits of Personality,* ed. A. Campbell and J. Gibbs (Oxford and Boston: Basil Blackwell, 1986).
36. Lejeune, "Management of a Mugging," p. 134.
37. J. Gibbs, "A Cognitive Model of Drinking and Public Disorder," paper presented at Drinking and Public Disorder Conference, Oxford University, November 1990, pp. 6–7.
38. Fortune, Vega, and Silverman, "Study of Female Robbers."
39. Luckenbill, "Generating Compliance."
40. Allen, *Assault with a Deadly Weapon,* p. 104.
41. Walsh, *Heavy Business;* Luckenbill, "Patterns of Force in Robbery," and "Generating Compliance."
42. J. D. Wright and P. H. Rossi, *Armed and Considered Dangerous: A Survey of Felons and Their Firearms* (New York: Aldine de Gruyter, 1986).
43. Male robbers are twice as likely as female robbers to inflict serious injuries, including rape and gunshot and knife wounds. This is probably associated with men's more frequent use of weapons and the specifically male nature of sexual assault as a crime "bonus." (See Harlow, *Special Report*; P. Cook and D. Nagin, *Does the Weapon Matter?* [Washington,

D.C.: Institute for Law and Social Research, 1979]; and Katz, *Seductions of Crime.*)

44. Lejeune, "Management of a Mugging."
45. Katz, *Seductions of Crime,* p. 247. (Emphasis added.)
46. Cook and Nagin, *Does the Weapon Matter?*
47. F. Feeney, "Robbers as Decision Makers," in *The Reasoning Criminal,* ed. D. Cornish and R. Clarke (New York: Springer-Verlag, 1986).
48. J. Chaiken and M. Chaiken, *Varieties of Criminal Behavior* (Santa Monica: Rand Corporation, 1982).
49. Wright and Rossi, *Armed and Considered Dangerous.*
50. Katz, *Seductions of Crime,* p. 215. (Emphasis added.)
51. Ibid.
52. Ibid., p. 216.
53. Allen, *Assault with a Deadly Weapon,* pp. 53, 104.
54. Ibid., p. 181.
55. Ibid., p. 184.
56. Lejeune, "Management of a Mugging," p. 140.
57. R. Block, *Violent Crime: Environment, Interaction and Death* (Lexington, Mass.: Lexington Books, 1977).
58. Cook, "Victim Resistance and Injury."
59. Block, *Violent Crime.*

7. Intimate Rage: Violence in Marriage

1. Statistics in this and the following paragraph are from M. A. Straus, R. J. Gelles, and S. K. Steinmetz, *Behind Closed Doors: Violence in the American Family* (New York: Doubleday/Anchor, 1980). For the results of a ten-year follow-up survey that produced similar findings, see M. A. Straus and R. J. Gelles, *Physical Violence in American Families: Risk Factors and Adaptations to Violence in 8,145 Families* (New Brunswick, N.J.: Transaction, 1990). See also J. M. Makepeace, "Courtship Violence Among College Students," *Family Relations* 30 (1981): 97–102; idem, "Life Events Stress and Courtship Violence," *Family Relations* 32 (1983): 101–9; J. L. Brutz and B. B. Ingoldsby, "Conflict Resolution in Quaker Families," *Journal of Marriage and the Family* 46 (1984): 21–26; W. H. Meredith, D. A. Abbott, and S. L. Adams, "Family Violence: Its Relation to Marital and Parental Satisfaction and Family Strengths," *Journal of Family Violence* 1 (1986): 299–305; M. E. Szinovacz, "Using Couple Data as a Methodological Tool: The Case of Marital Violence,"

Journal of Marriage and the Family 45 (1983): 633–44; J. Barling, K. D. O'Leary, E. N. Jouriles, D. Vivian, and K. E. MacEwen, "Factor Similarity of the Conflict Tactics Scale Across Samples, Spouses and Sites: Issues and Implications," *Journal of Family Violence* 2, no. 1 (1987): 37–55.

2. H. Lerner, *The Dance of Anger* (New York: Harper and Row, 1985); J. Miller, *Toward a New Psychology of Women*, 2d ed. (Boston: Beacon Press, 1986); J. Stets, *Domestic Violence and Control* (New York: Springer-Verlag, 1988); L. H. Bowker, *Beating Wife Beating* (Lexington, Mass.: Lexington Books, 1983); L. Walker, *The Battered Woman Syndrome* (New York: Springer-Verlag, 1984); D. G. Dutton, *The Domestic Assault of Women: Psychological and Criminal Justice Perspectives* (Boston: Allyn and Bacon, 1988).
3. See C. Gilligan, *In a Different Voice: Psychological Theory and Women's Development* (Cambridge, Mass.: Harvard University Press, 1982).
4. K. H. Coleman, M. L. Weinman, and B. P. Hsi, "Factors Affecting Conjugal Violence," *Journal of Psychology* 105 (1980): 197–202; J. A. Fagan, D. K. Stewart, and K. V. Hanson, "Violent Men or Violent Husbands?" in *The Dark Side of Families: Current Family Violence Research*, ed. D. Finkelhor, R. J. Gelles, G. T. Hotaling, and M. A. Straus (Beverly Hills, Calif.: Sage, 1983); D. S. Kalmuss, "The Intergenerational Transmission of Family Aggression," *Journal of Marriage and the Family* 46, no. 1 (1984): 11–19; A. Rosenbaum and K. D. O'Leary, "Marital Violence: Characteristics of Abusive Couples," *Journal of Consulting and Clinical Psychology* 49 (1981): 63–71; D. Sonkin and M. Durphy, *Learning to Live Without Violence: A Handbook for Men* (San Francisco: Volcano Press, 1985); B. Star, "Comparing Battered and Non-battered Women," *Victimology* 3, nos. 1–2 (1978): 32–44; Straus, Gelles, and Steinmetz, *Behind Closed Doors*.
5. G. T. Hotaling and D. B. Sugarman, "An Analysis of Risk Markers in Husband to Wife Violence: The Current State of Knowledge," *Violence and Victims* 1, no. 2 (1986): 101–24; Kalmuss, "Intergenerational Transmission of Family Aggression"; Rosenbaum and O'Leary, "Marital Violence."
6. R. E. Dobash and R. P. Dobash, *Violence Against Wives* (New York: Free Press, 1979), p. 151.
7. L. Walker, *The Battered Woman* (New York: Harper and Row, 1979), p. 83.
8. Ibid., p. 117.
9. Ibid., p. 91.
10. Dobash and Dobash, *Violence Against Wives*, p. 129.

11. F. McNulty and F. Hughes, *The Burning Bed* (New York: Harcourt, Brace, Jovanovich, 1980).
12. M. D. Pagelow, *Family Violence* (New York: Praeger, 1984); J. Fagan and A. Browne, "Marital Violence: Physical Aggression Between Women and Men in Intimate Relationships," paper commissioned by the Panel on Understanding and Control of Violent Behavior (Washington, D.C.: National Academy of Sciences, 1990).
13. I. H. Frieze and A. Browne, "Violence in Marriage," in *Family Violence,* ed. L. Ohlin and M. Tonry (*Crime and Justice: An Annual Review of Research,* vol. 11) (Chicago: University of Chicago Press, 1989), pp. 163–218.
14. See G. K. Kantor and M. A. Straus, "The 'Drunken Bum' Theory of Wife Beating," *Social Problems* 34, no. 3 (1987): 213–30; Fagan and Browne, "Marital Violence"; S. P. Taylor, C. B. Gammon, and D. R. Capasso, "Aggression as a Function of the Interaction of Alcohol and Threat," *Journal of Personality and Social Psychology* 34 (1976): 938–41; J. Fagan, "Intoxication and Aggression," in *Drugs and Crime,* ed. J. Q. Wilson and M. Tonry (*Crime and Justice: An Annual Review of Research,* vol. 13) (Chicago: University of Chicago Press, 1990); K. Pernanen, "Alcohol and Crimes of Violence," in *The Biology of Alcoholism: Social Aspects of Alcoholism,* ed. B. Kissin and H. Begleiter (New York: Plenum, 1976); idem, "Theoretical Aspects of the Relationship Between Alcohol Use and Crime," in *Drinking and Crime,* ed. J. J. Collins (New York: Plenum, 1981); Bowker, *Beating Wife Beating.*
15. E. Stark, A. Flitcraft, and W. Frazier, "Medicine and Patriarchal Violence: The Social Construction of a Private Event," *International Journal of Health Services* 9 (1979): 461–93.
16. Although this is partly because women rarely inflict real injury on their partners, there are other forces at work. The problem of wife beating has been publicized by women's groups whose mission is to draw attention to the injustices and abuses that women experience on a daily basis. In a sense they have come to own the problem. Those who do research and allocate funds in this area are acutely sensitive to women's issues. Wife beating has become so intimately bound up with feminist ideology that there is a real reluctance to focus upon the other side of the coin—physical aggression by wives. Few seriously challenge the figures—replicated time and time again—indicating that men and women commit similar numbers of violent acts in the home.

    The thrust of the objection to pursuing research on women's aggression is that it tends to imply that men and women are equally dangerous to one another. When Suzanne Steinmetz wrote an article entitled "The Battered Husband Syndrome," she was attacked by many academics for focusing on women's aggression while failing to highlight the far more dangerous injuries inflicted by men. A second line of feminist opinion suggests that aggression by wives occurs only in self-defense against their husbands. There are no data that directly supports this position. Among couples who report domestic violence, one-quarter are situations in which only the woman is the aggressor. Extrapolating from fairly inadequate data, one expert estimates that about half of wives' aggression occurs in self-defense.

However distasteful it may be politically to some ideological stakeholders, women are not only victims. They are as capable as men of being aggressors. What is perhaps surprising is the absence of domestic aggression by the vast majority of women who are subject to the double and conflicting demands of work and home, with initiative and competitiveness demanded by one and subservience and cooperation required by the other. To deny the legitimacy of studying women's aggression in the home is a sad loss for our understanding of aggression, but, equally important, it does a grave injustice to women to recognize them only as victims rather than as active agents. By stereotyping them as helpless and passive, we sorely underestimate and oversimplify their complex and often conflicted sense of their own rights. Because of the taboo on researching the nature of women's domestic aggression, the data on which I base my argument in this section are considerably thinner than the information that is available about men. (See S. Steinmetz, "The Battered Husband Syndrome," *Victimology* 2 [1978]: 499–509; E. Pleck, J. H. Pleck, M. Grossman, and P. B. Bart, "The Battered Data Syndrome: A Comment on Steinmetz's Article," *Victimology* 2 [1978]: 680–83; W. Breines and L. Gordon, "Review Essay: The New Scholarship on Family Violence," *Signs: Journal of Women in Culture and Society* 8 [1983]: 490–531; C. Greenblat, "A Hit Is a Hit Is a Hit . . . or Is It? Approval and Tolerance of the Use of Physical Force by Spouses," in *The Dark Side of Families,* ed. Finkelhor et al., pp. 235–60; D. G. Saunders, "When Battered Women Use Violence: Husband-abuse or Self-defense?" *Violence and Victims* 1 [1986]: 47–60; R. A. Berk, S. F. Berk, D. R. Loseke, and D. Rauma, "Mutual Combat and Other Family Violence Myths," in *The Dark Side of Families,* ed. Finkelhor et al.; M. A. Straus, "Victims and Aggressors in Marital Violence," *American Behavioral Scientist* 23 [1980]: 681–704.)

17. J. Archer and B. Lloyd, *Sex and Gender* (Cambridge: Cambridge University Press, 1982); W. Gove and J. Tudor, "Adult Sex Roles and Mental Illness," *American Journal of Sociology* 78 (1973): 812–35; I. Al-Issa, "Gender and Adult Psychopathology," in *Gender and Psychopathology,* ed. I. Al-Issa (New York: Academic Press, 1982).
18. D. Sanders and J. Reed, *Kitchen Sink or Swim?* (Harmondsworth, U.K.: Penguin Books, 1982).
19. L. Davidson and L. Gordon, *The Sociology of Gender* (Chicago: Rand McNally, 1979).
20. A. Oakley, *The Sociology of Housework* (London: Martin Robertson, 1974).
21. Ibid., p. 45.
22. Straus, Gelles, and Steinmetz, *Behind Closed Doors.*
23. Ibid.
24. Sanders and Reed, *Kitchen Sink or Swim?* p. 150.
25. Women also take on men's emotional work for them. Because men are particularly vulnerable to threats to their self-esteem, they often avoid discussing events they construe as demeaning. Women will often rush into this masculine emotional void and take over the role of expresser. In this way a wife can express solidarity with her husband, display her empathy for him, and reaffirm that everything that happens to him happens to her too. But as the husband comes to depend upon this vicarious emotionality, the wife increases the load of stress that she absorbs on his behalf. She must cope not only with her own disappointments but with his as well, and this takes a toll in her day-to-day stress level. (Lerner, *The Dance of Anger.*)
26. Dobash and Dobash, *Violence Against Wives,* p. 119.
27. Ibid.
28. Sanders and Reed, *Kitchen Sink or Swim?* p. 149.
29. D. Tannen, *You Just Don't Understand: Women and Men in Conversation* (New York: Morrow, 1990).
30. Dobash and Dobash, *Violence Against Wives.*
31. Sanders and Reed, *Kitchen Sink or Swim?* p. 159.
32. Tannen, *You Just Don't Understand,* chap. 1.
33. Ibid., chap. 3.
34. M. A. Straus, "Social Stress and Marital Violence in a National Sample of American Families," in *Physical Violence in American Families,* ed. Straus and Gelles.
35. J. Stets, "Verbal and Physical Aggression in Marriage," *Journal of Marriage and the Family* 52 (1990): 501–14; quotation is on p. 512.

36. A. Browne, *When Battered Women Kill* (New York: Free Press, 1987).
37. E. Goffman, *Interaction Ritual* (Garden City, N.Y.: Doubleday, 1967).
38. K. Deaux and B. Major, "Putting Gender into Context: An Interactive Model of Gender-Related Behavior," *Psychological Bulletin* 94 (1987): 369–89.
39. D. Fitz and S. Gerstenzang, "Anger in Everyday Life: When, Where and with Whom?" (St. Louis: University of Missouri-St. Louis, 1978. ERIC Document Reproduction Service No. ED 160 966); J. Averill, *Anger and Aggression* (New York: Springer-Verlag, 1982).
40. Straus, Gelles, and Steinmetz, *Behind Closed Doors.*
41. See Straus and Gelles, *Physical Violence in American Families.*
42. Straus, Gelles, and Steinmetz, *Behind Closed Doors;* Fagan and Browne, "Marital Violence." But see also C. Widom, "The Intergenerational Transmission of Violence," in *Pathways to Criminal Violence,* ed. N. Weiner and M. Wolfgang (Newbury Park, Calif.: Sage, 1988).
43. Straus and Gelles, *Physical Violence in American Families.*
44. This social judgment explanation of women's adaptation to stress is based upon that of Angela Browne in *When Battered Women Kill.*
45. Tannen, *You Just Don't Understand;* Lerner, *The Dance of Anger.*
46. M. Straus and R. Gelles, "How Violent Are American Families? Estimates from the National Family Violence Surveys and Other Studies," in *Physical Violence in American Families,* ed. Straus and Gelles.
47. Walker, *The Battered Woman,* p. 97.
48. Straus and Gelles, "How Violent Are American Families?"
49. E. W. Gondolf, *Men Who Batter; An Integrated Approach to Wife Beating* (Holmes Beach, Fla.: Learning Publications, 1985), p. 71.
50. R. Gelles, *The Violent Home: A Study of Physical Aggression Between Husbands and Wives* (Newbury Park, Calif.: Sage, 1974).
51. Dobash and Dobash, *Violence Against Wives,* p. 133.
52. Gelles, *The Violent Home,* p. 139.
53. Walker, *The Battered Woman,* pp. 100–101.
54. Browne, *When Battered Women Kill.*
55. Walker, *The Battered Woman,* pp. 84–85.
56. Bowker, *Beating Wife Beating.*
57. Dobash and Dobash, *Violence Against Wives,* chap. 8.
58. R. A. Berk, D. R. Loseke, S. F. Berk, and D. Rauma, "Bringing the Cops Back In: A Study of Efforts to Make the Criminal Justice System More Responsive to Incidents of Family Violence," *Social Science Research* 9 (1980): 193–215; D. Black, *The Manners and Customs of Police* (New

York: Academic Press, 1980); D. A. Ford, "Wife Battery and Criminal Justice: A Study of Victim Decision Making," *Family Relations* 32 (1983): 463–75; N. Loving, *Responding to Spouse Abuse and Wife Beating: A Guide for Police* (Washington, D.C.: Police Executive Research Forum, 1980); G. K. Kantor and M. A. Straus, "Response of Victims and the Police to Assaults on Wives," in *Behind Closed Doors,* ed. Straus, Gelles, and Steinmetz.

59. M. Schulman, *A Survey of Spousal Violence Against Women in Kentucky* (Frankfort, Ky.: Kentucky Commission on the Status of Women, 1979); D. A. Gaguin, "Spouse Abuse: Data from the National Crime Survey," *Victimology* 2, nos. 3–4 (1978): 632–42.
60. M. E. Wolfgang, *Patterns in Criminal Homicide* (New York: Wiley, 1958); Browne, *When Battered Women Kill;* M. E. Wolfgang, "Husband-Wife Homicides," *Journal of Social Therapy,* 4th qtr. (1956): 263–71.
61. K. Lindsey, "When Battered Women Strike Back: Murder or Self-Defense?" *Viva* (September 1978): 58–59, 66–74.
62. Wolfgang, *Patterns in Criminal Homicide.*
63. Browne, *When Battered Women Kill;* A. Jones, *Women Who Kill* (New York: Fawcett Columbine Books, 1980); P. D. Chimbos, *Marital Violence: A Study of Inter-spousal Homicide* (San Francisco: R and E Research Associates, 1978); J. Totman, *The Murderess: A Psychosocial Study of Criminal Homicide* (San Francisco: R and E Research Associates, 1978).
64. Lindsey, "When Battered Women Strike Back."
65. Wolfgang, *Patterns in Criminal Homicide.*
66. McNulty and Hughes, *The Burning Bed,* p. 164.
67. Browne, *When Battered Women Kill.*
68. Ibid., p. 154.
69. J. Katz, *Seductions of Crime: Moral and Sensual Attractions of Doing Evil* (New York: Basic Books, 1988).
70. D. J. Sonkin, D. Martin, and L. E. Walker, *The Male Batterer: A Treatment Approach* (New York: Springer-Verlag, 1985); D. G. Saunders and S. T. Azar, "Treatment Programs for Family Violence," in *Family Violence,* ed. L. Ohlin and M. Tonry (*Crime and Justice: An Annual Review of Research,* vol. 11) (Chicago: University of Chicago Press, 1989); M. J. Eddy and T. Myers, *Helping Men Who Batter: A Profile of Programs in the United States* (Texas Council on Family Violence, 1984).

8. Street Gangs

1. H. Asbury, *The Gangs of New York* (New York: Capricorn Books, 1970; orig. pub. 1927); F. Thrasher, *The Gang* (Chicago: Chicago University Press, 1927).
2. W. Miller, *Violence by Youth Gangs and Youth Groups as a Crime Problem in Major American Cities* (Washington, D.C.: U.S. Government Printing Office, 1975).
3. A. Cohen, *Delinquent Boys: The Culture of the Gang* (Glencoe, Ill.: Free Press, 1955); J. Short and F. Strodtbeck, *Group Process and Gang Delinquency* (Chicago: University of Chicago Press, 1965); R. Rice, "A Reporter at Large: The Persian Queens," *The New Yorker* 39 (1963): 135; see A. Campbell, "Female Participation in Street Gangs," in *Gangs in America,* ed. R. Huff (Newbury Park, Calif.: Sage, 1990).
4. K. Hanson, *Rebels in the Streets: The Story of New York's Girl Gangs* (Englewood Cliffs, N.J.: Prentice-Hall, 1964); Welfare Council of New York City, *Working with Teenage Groups: A Report on the Central Harlem Project* (New York: Welfare Council of New York City, 1950).
5. F. Adler, *Sisters in Crime: The Rise of the New Female Criminal* (New York: McGraw-Hill, 1975); see also P. Giordano and S. Cernkovich, "On Complicating the Relationship Between Liberation and Delinquency," *Social Problems* 26 (1979): 467–81.
6. S. Norland, R. Wessel, and N. Shover, "Masculinity and Delinquency," *Criminology* 19 (1981): 421–33; W. Thornton, "Self-concept as a Mediating Factor in Delinquency," *Adolescence* 17 (1982): 749–68.
7. J. Fagan, "Social Processes of Delinquency and Drug Use Among Urban Gangs," in *Gangs in America,* ed. R. Huff; M. Klein and C. Maxson, "Street Gang Violence," in *Violent Crime, Violent Criminals,* ed. N. Weiner and M. Wolfgang (Newbury Park, Calif.: Sage, 1989); P. Tracy, *Subcultural Delinquency: A Comparison of the Incidence and Seriousness of Gang and Nongang Member Offensivity* (Philadelphia: University of Pennsylvania, Center of Studies in Criminology and Criminal Law, 1979); M. Morash, "Gangs and Violence," in *Violent Criminal Behavior,* ed. A. Reiss, N. Weiner, and J. Roth (Washington, D.C.: National Academy Press, 1990).
8. Klein and Maxson, "Street Gang Violence," p. 218.
9. Evidence for the contribution of handgun availability to the rise in serious gang violence is discussed in Klein and Maxson, "Street Gang Violence," and Morash, "Gangs and Violence"; see also J. Moore, "Variations in Violence Among Hispanic Gangs," in *Violence and Homicide in Hispanic Communities,* ed. J. Kraus (Washington, D.C.: National Institute

of Mental Health, 1987). The media explanation of the increasingly lethal nature of gang violence is gangs' involvement in selling drugs. Their violence is allegedly instrumental in running their crime organization. Los Angeles gangs, they assert, have formed themselves into two factions—the Crips and the Bloods—that are involved in drug import and distribution across the nation. Gangs have metamorphosed from local territorial groups into national business organizations. Researchers, however, dispute this interpretation. Gang members have been involved in street-level drug sales for many years. In the 1940s and 1950s, Chicano gang members were heavily involved in heroin use and sales, and marijuana selling has long been a source of income for gang members dealing on street corners. Large-scale surveys show that about 34 percent of male gang members (compared with 9 percent of other local youths) deal drugs. But these studies also show that selling is done by individuals or small groups rather than being an orchestrated gang activity.

As for the migration of big-city gangs into smaller cities, there is little evidence that this is motivated by organized drug trafficking. A careful study of the Illinois scene examined the two gang "nations" of the People and the Folks in Chicago. Their emergence in Milwaukee was first thought to be another example of organized gang expansion, but in fact it was local youth mimicking the Chicago pattern to gain notoriety. It is likely that the same thing has happened on the West Coast. Local groups of drug sellers can capitalize on the Los Angeles names to scare off the competition. Most important, studies that have focused on gang members themselves find little support for an association between drug selling and higher rates of violence. A study of three major cities found many gangs who dealt drugs but were not especially violent. A Los Angeles study found no relationship between the number of gang members who sold drugs and deaths in gang warfare. In fact it was *nongang* homicides that were most likely to be drug-related. (See "Armed, Sophisticated and Violent: Two Drug Gangs Blanket Nation," *New York Times,* November 25, 1988, A1; "In the Middle of LA's Gang Warfare," *New York Times* Magazine, May 22, 1988, 30; J. Moore, "Isolation and Stigmatization in the Development of an Underclass: The Case of Chicano Gangs in East Los Angeles," *Social Problems* 33 [1985]: 1–30; J. Fagan, "The Social Organization of Drug Use and Drug Dealing Among Urban Gangs," *Criminology* 27 [1989]: 633–70; J. Hagedorn and P. Macon, *People and Folks: Gangs, Crime and the Underclass in a Rustbelt City* [Chicago: Lakeview Press, 1988]; M. Klein, C. Maxson, and L. Cunningham, *Gang Involvement in Cocaine "Rock" Traf-*

ficking [Los Angeles: Center for Research on Crime and Social Control, Social Science Research Institute, 1988].)

10. W. Miller, "Violent Crime in City Gangs," *The Annals of the American Academy of Social and Political Sciences* 264 (1966): 96–112; M. Klein, *Street Gangs and Street Workers* (Englewood Cliffs, N.J.: Prentice-Hall, 1971).
11. P. Cook, "The Role of Firearms in Violent Crime: An Interpretive Review of the Literature," in *Criminal Violence,* ed. M. Wolfgang and N. Weiner (Beverly Hills, Calif.: Sage, 1982).
12. M. Hindelang, "With a Little Help from Their Friends: Group Participation in Reported Delinquent Behavior," *British Journal of Criminology* 16 (1976): 109–25; T. Hirschi, *Causes of Delinquency* (Berkeley: University of California Press, 1969).
13. Klein, *Street Gangs and Street Workers.*
14. R. Cloward and L. Ohlin, *Delinquency and Opportunity* (Glencoe, Ill.: Free Press, 1960); Cohen, *Delinquent Boys;* Short and Strodtbeck, *Group Process and Gang Delinquency.*
15. J. Wilson, *The Truly Disadvantaged: The Inner City, the Underclass and Public Policy* (Chicago: University of Chicago Press, 1987); Hagedorn and Macon, *People and Folks.*
16. Hirschi, *Causes of Delinquency*; M. Gottfredson and T. Hirschi, *A General Theory of Crime* (Stanford: Stanford University Press, 1990).
17. J. Moore, *Homeboys: Gangs, Drugs and Prison in the Barrios of Los Angeles* (Philadelphia: Temple University Press, 1978); J. Vigil, *Barrio Gangs: Street Life and Identity in Southern California* (Austin: University of Texas Press, 1988).
18. M. Brake, *Comparative Youth Culture: The Sociology of Youth Culture and Youth Subcultures in America, Britain and Canada* (London: Routledge and Kegan Paul, 1985); D. Hebdige, *Subculture: The Meaning of Style* (London: Methuen, 1979); K. Pryce, *Endless Pressure* (Middlesex, U.K.: Penguin, 1979); E. Copferson, *La Génération de Blousons Noirs* (Paris: Maspero, 1961); J. Monad, "Juvenile Gangs in Paris: Toward a Structural Analysis," *Journal of Research in Crime and Delinquency* 4 (1967): 142–65.
19. S. Hall and T. Jefferson, *Resistance Through Rituals* (London: Hutchinson, 1976); P. Willis, *Learning to Labour* (Farnborough, U.K.: Saxon House, 1977); D. Hargreaves, *Social Relations in a Secondary School* (London: Routledge and Kegan Paul, 1967).
20. W. Whyte, *Street Corner Society: The Social Structure of an Italian Slum* (Chicago: University of Chicago Press, 1943).

21. D. Luckenbill, "Criminal Homicide as a Situated Transaction," *Social Problems* 25 (1977): 176–86.
22. L. Curtis, *Violence, Race and Culture* (Lexington, Mass.: Lexington Books, 1975).
23. A fuller account can be found in A. Campbell, *The Girls in the Gang*, 2d ed. (Oxford and Boston: Basil Blackwell, 1990). Quotations from female gang members are from the research reported in this book.
24. J. Moore, "Changing Chicano Gangs: Acculturation, Generational Change, Evolution of Deviance or Emerging Underclass?" in *Proceedings of the Conference on Comparative Ethnicity*, ed. J. Johnson and M. Oliver (Los Angeles: University of California at Los Angeles Institute for Social Science Research, 1988).

9. Women's Aggression and the Male Establishment

1. H. Arendt, *On Violence* (New York: Harcourt Brace and World, 1970), p. 56.
2. S. Lukes, *Power: A Radical View* (London: Macmillan, 1974).
3. Ibid., p. 24.
4. K. Davis, M. Leijenaar, and J. Oldersma, *The Gender of Power* (London: Sage, 1991).
5. D. Zillmann, *Hostility and Aggression* (Hillsdale, N.J.: Erlbaum, 1979).
6. K. O'Donovan, "Defenses for Battered Women Who Kill," *Journal of Law and Society* 18, no. 2 (1991): 219–40.
7. C. P. Ewing, *Battered Women Who Kill: Psychological Self-defense as Legal Justification* (Lexington, Mass.: Lexington Books, 1987).
8. *The Independent*, August 1, 1991 (London).
9. O'Donovan, "Defenses for Battered Women."
10. C. K. Gillespie, *Justifiable Homicide: Battered Women, Self-defense and the Law* (Columbus: Ohio State University Press, 1989).
11. A. Jones, *Women Who Kill* (New York: Fawcett Columbine, 1980).
12. O'Donovan, "Defenses for Battered Women."
13. State v. Wanrow, 88 Wash 2d 221, 559, P.2d 548 (1977).
14. A. Browne, *When Battered Women Kill* (New York: Macmillan/Free Press, 1987).
15. E. M. Schneider and S. B. Jordan, "Representation of Women Who Defend Themselves in Response to Physical or Sexual Assault," *Women's Rights Law Reporter* 4, no. 3 (1978): 149–63; quotation is on p. 153.

16. E. Hilberman and K. Munson, "Sixty Battered Women," *Victimology* 2 (1977): 464.
17. "Battered Wife Who Set Fire to Husband Wins Right to Retrial," *London Times,* August 1, 1992; "Women Wins Murder Case Retrial," *The Independent,* August 1, 1992 (London).
18. L. Walker, *The Battered Woman* (New York: Harper and Row, 1979); L. Walker, R. Thyfault, and A. Browne, "Beyond the Jurors' Ken: Battered Women," *Vermont Law Reporter* 7 (1982): 1–14.
19. M. E. P. Seligman, *Helplessness: On Depression, Development and Death* (San Francisco: Freeman, 1975).
20. Ewing, *Battered Women Who Kill.*
21. H. Allen, *Justice Unbalanced* (Milton Keynes, England: Open University Press, 1988); U. Padel and P. Stevenson, *Insiders: Women's Experience of Prison* (London: Virago, 1988).
22. Personal communication, Women in Special Hospitals, 25 Horsell Rd., London.
23. Ibid.
24. K. Dalton, *Once a Month* (London: Fontana, 1978), p. 11.
25. S. Blumenthal and C. Nadelson, "Late Luteal Phase Dysphoric Disorder (Premenstrual Syndrome): Clinical Implications," *Journal of Clinical Psychiatry* 49 (1988): 469–74.
26. G. A. Sampson, "Premenstrual Syndrome: A Double-Blind Controlled Trial of Progesterone and Placebo," *British Journal of Psychiatry* 135 (1979): 209–15; J. W. Taylor, "Plasma Progesterone, Oestradiol 17 Beta and Premenstrual Symptoms," *Acta Psychiatrica Scandinavia* 60 (1979): 76–86.
27. R. T. Frank, "The Hormonal Causes of Premenstrual Tension," *Archives of Neurology and Psychiatry* 26 (1931): 1053–57.
28. M. B. Parlee, "The Premenstrual Syndrome," *Psychological Bulletin* 80 (1973): 454–65; P. Caplan, J. McCurdy-Myers, and M. Gans, "Should Premenstrual Syndrome Be Called a Psychiatric Abnormality?" *Feminism and Psychology* 2 (1992): 27–44.
29. Dalton, *Once a Month,* p. 25.
30. Blumenthal and Nadelson, "Late Luteal Phase."
31. Dalton, *Once a Month,* pp. 97–100.
32. R. K. D. Koeske, "Theoretical-Conceptual Implications of Study Design and Statistical Analyses: Research on the Menstrual Cycle," in *Sex Roles: Origins, Influences and Implications for Women,* ed. C. Stark-Adamec (Montreal: Eden, 1980); M. B. Parlee, "On PMS and Psychiatric Abnor-

mality," *Feminism and Psychology* 2 (1992): 105–8; idem, "The Premenstrual Syndrome."

33. Dalton, *Once a Month.*
34. B. S. Kopell, D. T. Lunde, R. B. Clayton, and R. H. Moos, "Variations in Some Measures of Arousal During the Menstrual Cycle," *Journal of Nervous and Mental Diseases* 148 (1969): 180–87.
35. E. E. Levitt and B. Lubin, "Some Personality Factors Associated with Menstrual Complaints and Menstrual Attitude," *Journal of Psychosomatic Research* 11 (1967): 267–70.
36. S. Silbergeld, N. Brast, and E. P. Nobel, "The Menstrual Cycle: A Double-Blind Study of Symptoms, Mood and Behavior and Biochemical Variables Using Enovid and Placebo," *Psychosomatic Medicine* 33 (1971): 411–28.
37. K. Dalton, *The Premenstrual Syndrome* (Springfield, Ill.: Charles C Thomas, 1964).
38. A. Lieber and C. Sherrin, "The Case of the Full Moon," *Human Behavior* 1 (1972): 29.
39. D. Ruble, "Premenstrual Symptoms: A Reinterpretation," *Science* 197 (1977): 291–92.
40. C. Bisson and C. Whissell, "Will Premenstrual Syndrome Produce a Ms. Hyde? Evidence from Daily Administrations of the Emotions Profile Index," *Psychological Reports* 65 (1989): 179–84; D. N. Ruble and J. Brooks-Gunn, "Menstrual Symptoms: A Social-Cognitive Analysis," *Journal of Behavioral Medicine* 2 (1979): 171–94.
41. M. B. Parlee, "Stereotypic Beliefs About Menstruation: A Methodological Note on the Moos Menstrual Distress Questionnaire and Some New Data," *Psychosomatic Medicine* 36 (1974): 229–40; L. Rees, "The Premenstrual Tension Syndrome," *British Medical Journal* 1 (1953): 1014–16; R. A. McCance, M. C. Luff, and E. E. Widdowson, "Physical and Emotional Periodicity in Women," *Journal of Hygiene* 37 (1937): 571–605; Kopell et al., "Variations in Some Measures of Arousal."
42. M. Paulson, "Psychological Concomitants of Premenstrual Tension," *American Journal of Obstetrics and Gynecology* 81 (1961): 733–38; M. Schuckit, V. Daly, G. Herrman, and S. Hineman, "Premenstrual Symptoms and Depression in a University Population," *Diseases of the Nervous System* 36 (1975): 516–17; S. Smith and C. Sauder, "Food Cravings, Depression and Menstrual Problems," *Psychosomatic Medicine* 31 (1969): 281–87; T. Kashiwagi, J. N. McClure, and R. D. Wetzel, "Premenstrual Affective Syndrome and Psychiatric Disorder," *Diseases of the*

Nervous System 37 (1976): 116–19; Blumenthal and Nadelson, "Late Luteal Phase"; Parlee, "The Premenstrual Syndrome."

43. A. Coppen and N. Kessel, "Menstruation and Personality," *British Journal of Psychiatry* 109 (1963): 711–21.
44. K. E. Paige, "Women Learn to Sing the Menstrual Blues," *Psychology Today* 7 (1973): 41–46.
45. I. Al-Issa, *Gender and Psychopathology* (London: Academic, 1982).
46. M. Davis, "Premenstrual Syndrome," in *Report of the Public Health Service Task Force on Women's Health*, vol. 2 (Washington, D.C.: U.S. Government Printing Office, 1985), pp. 80–85; see also G. Robinson, "Premenstrual Syndrome: Current Knowledge and Management," *Canadian Medical Association Journal* 140 (1989): 605–10.
47. D. Spender, *Invisible Women: The Schooling Scandal* (London: Writers and Readers Publishing Cooperative, 1982); L. C. Wilkinson and C. B. Marrett, *Gender Influences in the Classroom* (New York: Academic Press, 1985).

INDEX